Jean Newton McIlwraith

The Children's Study

Canada

Jean Newton McIlwraith

The Children's Study
Canada

ISBN/EAN: 9783337186401

Printed in Europe, USA, Canada, Australia, Japan

Cover: Foto ©ninafisch / pixelio.de

More available books at **www.hansebooks.com**

THE CHILDREN'S
STUDY

CANADA

THE CHILDREN'S STUDY

SCOTLAND. By Mrs. OLIPHANT.

IRELAND. Edited by R. BARRY O'BRIEN.

ENGLAND. By FRANCES E. COOKE.

GERMANY. By KATE FREILIGRATH KROEKER.

OLD TALES FROM GREECE. By ALICE ZIMMERN.

FRANCE. By MARY C. ROWSELL.

ROME. By MARY FORD.

SPAIN. By LEONARD WILLIAMS.

CANADA. By J. N. MCILWRAITH.

MONUMENT TO CHAMPLAIN.
UNVEILED AT QUEBEC, SEPTEMBER, 1898

The Children's Study

CANADA

BY

J. N. McILWRAITH

TORONTO
WILLIAM BRIGGS
1899

QUEBEC

[All rights reserved.]

ONTARIO

CONTENTS

PART FIRST
TO THE END OF THE SIXTEENTH CENTURY

CHAPTER I
THE FIRST PEOPLE OF CANADA . . .	PAGE I

CHAPTER II
THE EARLIEST VISITORS 13

CHAPTER III
THE VOYAGES OF JACQUES CARTIER AND OTHERS 24

PART SECOND
TO THE END OF THE SEVENTEENTH CENTURY

CHAPTER IV
THE ROMANCE OF ACADIA . . 35

CHAPTER V
THE FATHER OF NEW FRANCE 49

CHAPTER VI
THE MISSIONARIES 62

CHAPTER VII
A ROYAL PROVINCE 74

CHAPTER VIII
FRONTENAC AND LA SALLE 88

PART THIRD
TO THE END OF THE EIGHTEENTH CENTURY

CHAPTER IX
NEW FRANCE SPREADS HER WINGS . . 102

CHAPTER X
THE FIGHT FOR NOVA SCOTIA . . . 115

CHAPTER XI
CANADA HOLDS HER OWN 127

CHAPTER XII
LOUISBOURG TO QUEBEC . . 140

CONTENTS

CHAPTER XIII
THE FIRST FEW YEARS OF BRITISH RULE ... 154

CHAPTER XIV
THE UNITED EMPIRE LOYALISTS . . . 166

PART FOURTH
TO THE END OF THE NINETEENTH CENTURY

CHAPTER XV
THE WAR OF 1812-14 179

CHAPTER XVI
MISGUIDED PATRIOTS 192

CHAPTER XVII
THE NEW DOMINION 204

CHAPTER XVIII
THE NORTH-WEST 215

CHAPTER XIX
BRITISH COLUMBIA 228

CHAPTER XX
'DAUGHTER AM I IN MY MOTHER'S HOUSE, BUT MISTRESS IN MY OWN' . . . 239

Dominion of Canada

PART FIRST

TO THE END OF THE SIXTEENTH CENTURY

CHAPTER I

THE FIRST PEOPLE OF CANADA

THE oldest Canadians are the Indians. For many hundreds of years before white men had set foot upon the western continent red men had found homes there, both in North and South America.

Where did they come from at the first?

Their high cheek-bones, Roman noses, small, deep-set eyes, and straight hair make them very unlike the darker, woolly-haired negroes from Africa, and very different also from the white-skinned races of Europe. It is among the Tartars and other wild tribes of Eastern Asia that are seen faces which might pass for North American Indians, and that is one reason why some of the men who have made a study of the subject think that the first people of America came from Asia.

The two continents are so close together up at the north-west, it is not hard to cross from one to the other on the ice at Behring Strait. Probably the Eskimos came that way. These natives are the same, whether on the Siberian or the Alaskan side of the Strait, and they occupy also the Arctic regions of North America, coming as far south as the shores of Hudson's Bay, and eastward to the coasts of Greenland and Labrador.

The name Eskimo is an Indian word, meaning "Eaters of raw flesh," and these people consume much fat and oil too, but very few vegetables. An Eskimo might pass for a white man if his face were washed, but he thinks that many layers of grease keep out the cold; and he does not believe in house-cleaning either. He is generally under five feet in height, has a flat, broad face, and a stay-at-home disposition. He would rather live in his snow hut up in the frozen north and hunt the whale and the walrus for his food and clothing than come southward to sunnier climes to quarrel with the Indian for his hunting grounds. It may have been the Indian who drove him up there in the first place, but most students think that the Eskimo was the last comer.

No one knows, but there are reasons for imagining, that if the people of Asia did cross to America they did not all come at once. There would be a family, perhaps, of one tribe driven from island to island of the Pacific Ocean which landed at last on some part of North or South America. This may have happened many ages ago, before the seas and the continents had settled into their present form, when there may have been less open water to cross. The currents of the Pacific Ocean run towards America, and most of the winds blow in that direction.

Whether landed by accident or driven out of their early homes by war or by want of food, it is probable that these emigrants settled some of the islands of the Pacific and came even so far as South America before the less fertile parts of Asia were filled up. The first people of America have been there a very long time. The earliest arrivals were not so wild and savage as the later lot. When the Spaniards landed on the coast of South America they were astonished at the wealth and cleverness of the natives, many relics of which are still to be seen. In North America it is the Mound-builders who have left traces of their work, even so far north as Lake Superior, where they worked the copper mines. The mounds of earth they threw up, and which one sees in different parts of the United States, may have been churches or burial-places, though they were more probably defences against their enemies. These enemies would likely be the first of the Indians, who would drive the Mound-builders farther and farther south, and at last put an end to them altogether.

These are some of the guesses white men have made on how the red men came to America, but nothing can be told with certainty about it, because the Indians of old could not write and did not keep any stories of their race in a form that can be understood by the people of to-day. We study the Indian skull, his religion, his language, his features, his habits, and some of us think he came from Asia, while some think he did not. All that is known for certain is that he was there when the first Europeans landed. Those bold sailors were looking for a passage to the East Indies, and when they found land where no land was known to be, they thought it must be some part of India, and so they called the natives Indians.

There were a great many different tribes, speaking a great many different tongues, but those that lived in the country now called Canada were mostly of the Algonquin family, who bore the name of Micmacs in Nova Scotia, Abenakis in New Brunswick, Ottawas and Montagnais in the province of Quebec, Ojibwas in Ontario, Blackfeet and Crees in the North-west. Tribes of the same family, settled farther south, used to till the soil, but the Canadian Algonquins lived by hunting, and when they had killed with their bows and arrows all the game birds, the deer, and the bears within a certain district they would roll up their tents, which were merely skins stretched on poles, and move elsewhere. Sometimes they moved for another cause—the Iroquois.

This was the family of Indians who lived to the south of Lake Ontario in what is now the northern part of the State of New York, between the Hudson and the Genesee rivers. There were five divisions of them, and therefore they were called the Five Nation

Indians — Mohawks, Oneidas, Onondagas, Cayugas, and Senecas. Though not nearly so large a family as the Algonquin, the Iroquois gained strength by their union, and they were the most fierce and cruel, as well as the bravest and wisest, of all the Indians. If they had joined hands with the Algonquins, instead of fighting them to the death, they might have kept the white men from settling this country for a century or two. But to go to war was the most important part of an Indian's life; he cared for nothing else; and the aim of the Iroquois was to kill off every other nation but his own five.

Family fights are always more bitter than those between strangers, and so the wars between the Iroquois and Hurons were the most savage on record because both belonged to the same stock. The Hurons, who lived between Lake Simcoe and Georgian Bay, made friends with the Algonquins to gain their help against the Iroquois, but the Neutral Nation would not join them. That family was also related to the Iroquois, and lived between Lake Erie and Lake Ontario. They were called neutral by the French because they did not side with either the Hurons or the Iroquois in their wars. It might have been safer for themselves to have joined the stronger party, because in the end the Iroquois killed or adopted the whole of them.

Captives from other nations kept up the number of the Iroquois, whose losses by war were, of course, very great. If a brave who went out to fight did not come back, his parents or his wife, his brother or his sister would usually adopt in his place one of the prisoners brought in by the war party, and this man would be bound to make his own the family which had thus saved him from a horrible death by torture, even though he should have to fight against his own friends ever afterwards. White men were sometimes adopted by the Indians in this way, and often they did not want to leave them, even when they had the chance.

The Hurons and Iroquois lived a more settled life than the Algonquins. They grew Indian corn around their villages and laid some of it up for winter use. Their houses were made so long that seven or eight families, and even so many as twenty could live under one roof. The sides of these lodges were made of long poles, slim enough to be bent together at the top, and to be placed also along the sides, crossways, to make a frame for the big pieces of bark that were tied on to keep out the rain and snow. The inside was a long, wide passage, with an open skylight the full length of the roof to let out the smoke, for down the middle were the fires, one between every two families, to warm them in winter and to cook their food all the year round. On either side, next the wall, was the long, low platform on which the Indians slept in the same clothes, made of the skins of animals, that they wore by day.

There was always a head man in each tribe, and he took counsel of others noted for being either great fighters or wise thinkers, but he never did more than advise or persuade the warriors. Each one could go on the war-path when he saw fit, alone or with two or three of his fellows, and the smaller the party the more glory was gained by the scalps they brought home. The custom of taking off the skin and top hair of an enemy arose, so say the Indians, at the time that a famous chief promised to give his beautiful daughter to the man who would bring him the dead body of the chief of another tribe, whom he hated. The young man who killed the enemy was hotly pursued by the friends of the dead chieftain when he was bringing him home to the living one to claim the reward, and as the body seemed to become heavier and heavier he cut it down lighter, bit by bit, till he arrived before his employer with only the scalp-lock in his hand. That was enough to show that he had done the deed.

Another custom of long standing among the Indians was the use of *wampum*, which was first made from bits of shells, but afterwards from beads got from white men. Necklaces of wampum were highly prized by warriors and squaws alike, and every clause of a treaty or agreement of any sort had to be sealed with a belt of wampum or it did not hold good. It was used as money too.

If a man killed one of his own tribe he was not killed himself, but was obliged to make presents of wampum and other things to the family of the man he had murdered. So when he wanted a wife he bought her from her father, and she became his drudge and slave for the rest of her life. It was the squaws who planted the corn when any was planted; they who made those marvels of lightness and toughness, the birch-bark canoes, as well as the bows and arrows for their lords, and carried the heaviest burdens at the *portages*. That name was given by the French to the places where canoes and all they contained had to be lifted out of the water and carried through the woods, to avoid rapids and waterfalls, or to reach the next one of the lakes and streams which were the only roads.

Indian babies were tied up between two stout strips of bark and carried about on their mothers' backs. Lame or sickly children died young—often helped out of the way. So were the old people, who sometimes begged their sons and daughters to make an end to them when they were no longer strong enough to endure the long, hard marches in search of food. In spite of these customs, the Indians were fond of their parents, their brothers and sisters, and indeed of the whole clan to which they belonged. This was shown in the strong, though useless, means they used to cure a sick person, the savage way they would fight to revenge one who was killed, and the care they took of the bodies of friends, after death.

Every ten or twelve years there was a great Feast of the Dead, when all the different clans of a tribe would bring the bones of their relations to one spot, where speeches would be made, relating how brave and how useful these people had been when alive. All the bones, as well as the bodies of more recent dead, would then be buried together in a deep pit lined with furs, and beside them would be placed bows and arrows, kettles, food, wampum, trinkets — anything that the spirits might be likely to need on their journey to the land of the hereafter. No Indian believed that a man died like a dog; he was more likely to believe that his dog lived for ever, like a man.

The natives on the Pacific coast of the continent are a lower type than the Eastern tribes. They flatten the heads of their children by tying boards on the front of their skulls while still soft, and when they grow up they seem to have no foreheads. The men are not tall and sinewy, like the tribes of the plains to the east of the Rocky Mountains, but are short and thick-set, with very strong arms, gained by generations of paddling, for they live chiefly by fishing. The boat is not the birch-bark canoe but the dug-out, made from a single log of one of the big trees of the country, and sometimes it is ornamented at the bow or stern by a rude carving of bird or beast. With a mild climate and plenty of fish and game near by, the "Siwash," as the British Columbia Indian is called, has never been such a rover nor such a fierce fighter as his brother to the eastward used to be.

Against all the scalping and burning and torturing that white men have suffered from

Indians must be placed the evil done to the red men by strong liquor and by the small-pox, both unknown before Europeans came. It must be remembered, too, how much the early settlers learned from them. The First Families never despaired of doing a thing for want of proper tools ; they made tools out of what was at hand, and that was the beginning of American cleverness at invention. The Indians taught them how to trap and to shoot fur-bearing animals, and to fish through holes in the ice ; how to follow a trail through the forest which ordinary eyes could not see, and how to find their way out if lost in the woods, by examining the bark of the trees to see on which side it grew thickest, for that was the north ; how to smoke tobacco and to grow potatoes; how to raise Indian corn under the standing forest trees to keep themselves from starving until such time as the fields needed for the smaller grains could be ploughed and planted, and how, in many ways to adapt themselves to the climate and circumstances of a new country.

QUEBEC

CHAPTER II

THE EARLIEST VISITORS

HOEVER first landed upon the western shores of the American continents, whether they came from China, Japan, Siberia, or from the islands of the Pacific Ocean, they did not go home and write, or have written for them, accounts of their voyages and the strange new lands they had seen. Of the earliest visitors to the eastern shores, on the other hand, there are records in plenty, some of them quite clear, others a little misty. Some describe wild men and animals, plants, mountains, rivers, and rocks, as they are now known

to have really been; while in others are fairy stories about palaces of gold and crystal, about one-legged men, griffins, hobgoblins, and demons that we know never existed.

The historical tales, and also the myths of the Northmen—a name given to the natives of Norway, Sweden, and Denmark—are called sagas, and from these old stories we learn that five hundred years before America was discovered by Columbus it had been visited by the Norsemen, or Northmen. These Vikings (Sons of the Fiord) were more at home on the sea than on land, and their "dragon" ships, with high, carved bows and sterns, propelled either by oars or sails, were both stronger and faster than the caravels of Columbus. About the year 875 they had settled upon Iceland, and to sail onwards to Greenland was a shorter journey than back to their homes in Scandinavia.

986. The saga of Eric the Red tells how he killed a man in Norway and fled to Iceland, got into trouble there and fled still further, sailing away to Greenland, where, with some comrades as hardy as himself, he spent three years in exploring the coasts. At last they fixed upon a good place for a settlement, near where Julianeshaab now stands, in a grassy valley at the head of Igaliko fiord. It was, and still is, one of the few spots that deserved the name *Greenland* Eric gave to it, which spread afterwards to the whole peninsula. He thought rightly that there was a great deal in a name, when one wanted to coax emigrants to a place. The first settlers from Iceland built their houses in the spot Eric had chosen, and called it Brattahlid. Other tiny villages sprang up near by in course of time, and a settlement was also planted on the west coast, so far north as Godthaab.

Eric the Red had several sons. Leif, the most famous of them, was a Christian, and brought the first priest to Greenland. The remains of a stone church built by the Norsemen can be seen at the present day, and they are said to have had several monasteries, a cathedral, and about a dozen churches for a population of five or six thousand.

Leif Ericson was much impressed by the story of one Bjarni Herjulfsson who told of losing his way in a mist while sailing between Iceland and Greenland, and of seeing land when the fog lifted, which was neither the one country nor the other, but lay further to the south and west. According to a writer of his own country, "Leif was a large man and strong, of noble aspect, prudent and moderate in all things," but he had his share of the daring spirit of his time, and though he had no mariner's compass, he made up his mind to search for this unknown country which Bjarni had seen.

1000. Thirty-five vikings sailed with Leif from Brattahlid, and truly they did find land before long, either Labrador or Newfoundland. Very desolate it looked, not like the fine wooded coast described by Bjarni, so they kept on farther to the south and came to a shore where the trees grew so thickly they named it Markland (Woodland). This was probably the coast of Cape Breton or Nova Scotia, so that Leif Ericson and his men were the first European visitors to Canada, so far as we know.

Sailing still southward, they landed at a place where many wild vines were growing, and they called it Vinland. There they spent the whole winter, which seemed mild to them after the climate of Greenland, but it was probably no further south than Massachusetts. From that time onward there were a number of expeditions from Greenland to Vinland, chiefly to bring home timber which was scarce both in Greenland and Iceland ; and some of the wood-cutters spent two or three winters in the new country, hewing down the tall trees that were to make masts for their ships.

Another saga relates how a rich nobleman, called Thorfinn Karlsefni, tried to found a colony in Vinland. He took cattle there, along with his settlers, and the natives were much alarmed at the bellowing of a bull, for they knew no domestic animal except the dog. Nor did they understand the value of the costly furs they sold to the Norsemen for little strips of red cloth, just as they gave them away to later explorers for beads and trinkets. Though friendly at first, it was not long before quarrels arose between the white men and the red, and the idea of planting a colony in Vinland had to be given up, for the Norsemen had not the firearms of a later day which gave Spanish, French, and English pioneers so great an advantage over hordes of savages armed only with bows and arrows.

Early in the fifteenth century the Greenland settlements were entirely forsaken, after an existence of four hundred years. It was most likely the Eskimo who destroyed them, though the decline of the shipping trade with Norway and Denmark, and a plague called the Black Death may have helped.

Nowhere else on the western continent are there any traces of the Norsemen remaining, though the walls of an old stone mill near Newport used to be thought their work. Longfellow's poem, "The Skeleton in Armor," was written with that idea, and it gives a good picture of one of those old vikings, but neither skeleton nor tower had in truth anything to do with the Norsemen.

Greenland in their day was considered but a remote part of Europe, and therefore they had no notion of the importance of their discovery. Believing, as they did, that the earth was flat, it might extend westward without end, for aught they knew, or cared. America had been discovered again for two hundred years before those who knew of the Norse sagas began to say, " This must be the country the Northmen called Vinland."

1394. An Italian, named Zeno, wrote an account of a visit he paid to the dying Norse settlements in Greenland, but with that exception there were no visitors to America from Europe (who left cards) for about one hundred years. The nations of the older continent had too many troubles at home to spend their strength in venturing abroad ; but peace brought plenty, and plenty brought the desire for luxuries that could be had only in the East. Trade revived, and India was the country every adventurer wanted to reach. Whoever should first succeed in sailing there, to bring home a ship-load of silks and diamonds, of gold and silver, sapphires and pearls, would be the most famous man in all Europe.

The Portuguese, who ranked next to the old Norsemen as mariners, tried it by sailing down the coast of Africa, even so far as the cape they named "Good Hope," because they were sure they had found the right way to reach India; and they had discovered most of the islands of the Atlantic Ocean before the Pacific was known to exist. Christopher Columbus went with the Portuguese on some of their voyages, but it was learning the wonderful lesson that the earth is round which decided him to sail directly westward in order to reach that eastern "land where the spices grow."

1492. The story of his going from court to court in Europe to find a sovereign with faith enough in his enterprise to fit out vessels for him is well known. So, too, is the glory he added to the reign of Ferdinand and Isabella by planting the Spanish flag upon San Salvador, one of the Bahama islands. Columbus thought it was an island off the coast of Japan which he had reached, and to the end of his life he believed that the different islands he discovered were not far from the clime he had come to seek. Therefore he called them the West Indies, and their natives, Indians.

Columbus made four voyages to the New World, but the year before he found the southern continent an English expedition had landed upon the mainland of North America. This was commanded by John Cabot, a Venetian by birth, but living with his family in Bristol, at that time the busiest seaport town of England.

Hearing the story of Columbus, and plenty of sailors' yarns besides, Master Cabot made up his mind to outdo them all. Nothing could be done without leave, in those days, so he had to get permission from Henry the Seventh before he could set out in search of new lands. He went at his own expense, and promised that one-fifth of the riches he might gain should be given to the English king.

1497. Generally two or three ships went together on these voyages into the unknown, but John Cabot sailed away to the westward with one small vessel and a crew of eighteen men, including probably his second son, Sebastian, a young man of twenty-four. They started in the beginning of May, and it was the 24th of June when they caught sight of the northern headland of Cape Breton, though they thought it was China. Cabot went ashore, and, according to the custom of discoverers, he set up the flag of the king who had sent him and took possession of the country in his name. No natives were seen, though some rude tools were found that must have been made by man.

It is not unlikely that the explorers sailed round the Gulf of St. Lawrence and out by the Straits of Belleisle, the best exit in the summer season. When they reached home, in the month of August, so great a stir did John Cabot make with the news he brought, that we are told he "dressed in silk and was called, or called himself 'the Great Admiral.'"

He and his son set out on a second trip in April of the next year, and they visited different points along the coast of North America, probably as far south as Cape Cod, but no one knows exactly, nor has any one told what became of John Cabot. His son, Sebastian, made other voyages alone, and is said to have entered the great inland sea, Hudson's Bay.

1500. The same shores touched upon by the Cabots were visited by Gaspar Cortereal in the interests of the King of Portugal. He brought back savages and white bears to Europe with him, but from his last voyage he never returned.

1504–1518. While the Spaniards were keeping up their search for gold in the south, fishermen from Normandy and Brittany were finding out the wealth more surely to be drawn in the shape of codfish from the Banks of Newfoundland. These are not land-banks but flat-topped mountains in the Atlantic Ocean whose heads come to within five hundred feet of the surface. Cape Breton was christened by Breton fishermen; but it was the Baron de Lèry who first tried to plant a colony in that region. He made a bad choice in Sable Island, off the coast of Nova Scotia, a bleak and barren spot noted ever since for its wrecks. His settlers all died, though their cattle lived on and multiplied.

Meanwhile the King of France woke up to what his neighbours of Europe were doing in the new West, and he cried—

"Shall the kings of Spain and Portugal divide all America between them without giving me a share? I should like to see the clause in Father Adam's will that makes them his sole heirs!"

1524. Francis the First therefore sent out a sailor of Florence, called Verrazano, to take what he could, and the parts taken seem to have been those already claimed by Cortereal and the Cabots; but it is not easy to say for certain, because each man made his own map and gave to the lands he saw what names he pleased. Very curious are these old charts, showing as they do that the early visitors never dreamt what a solid bulk of continent was between them and Asia. For long years they thought they were discovering islands through which, sooner or later, the desired passage to the Indies would be found, but after all Vasco da Gama got there first by sailing round the Cape of Good Hope (1497).

The coast-line of North America was not discovered as a whole, but just a scrap here and a scrap there. We see from maps made even in the middle of the sixteenth century that South America had been sailed about, and its size and shape pretty well known while North America was still thought to consist of islands.

First Brazil, then the whole of South America, and lastly North America were named from the famous pilot and astronomer, Americus Vespucius, a friend of Columbus, who made several voyages to both continents in the early years of the sixteenth century. He did what no one before him had done—wrote about the Western Hemisphere when he came back from it—and he was also the first to speak of a New World, as distinct from the Old World which Columbus and all the others thought they had found.

MANITOBA

CHAPTER III

THE VOYAGES OF JACQUES CARTIER AND OTHERS

ST. MALO on the northern coast of France is famed for its sailors, and there was born on December 31, 1494, one called Jacques Cartier. He went to sea when only a boy, but he was a man of forty ere he set out upon the voyage which has handed down his name. Before that he had been a "corsair," roaming the high seas in search of weaker vessels to capture, generally, though not always, those of the nation with which his own chanced to be at war. Cartier's ideas of right and wrong were never very clear, but he was a brave sailor. Picture one

going to sea in a vessel smaller than most modern yachts, and sailing in it not over a well-known route where thousands of ships have been before him, but over a pathless waste of waters, at a time of the world's history when men peopled the unknown with all sorts of terrible creatures.

1534. Francis the First, the same king who had sent out Verrazano, ten years before, gave Cartier leave to go, and he took with him one hundred and sixty-two men on his two little vessels, sailing from St. Malo on the 20th of April. Three weeks later he sighted Newfoundland about Bonavista Bay, and put into a harbour close by to have his ships repaired. Then he sailed northward near to an island completely covered with birds, or so it seemed, and swimming towards it, to feast upon them, was a huge bear "as white as any swan."

Cartier and his company went onwards to the coast of Labrador, which looked so dreary, even in the month of June, they were sure it must be the land, told of in the Bible, that was set apart for Cain; and the natives were unfriendly enough to have been his descendants. Through the Straits of Belleisle went the two little ships, sailing southwards, across the Gulf of St. Lawrence, till the end of Prince Edward Island came into view; thence into the Miramichi Bay, where so many savages paddled out in their canoes to see the wonderful strangers in boats moving with wings, that Cartier had to fire his cannon to scare them away; but the next day he went on shore and made friends with the chief of the Indians by giving him a red hat.

The next bay they entered was much larger, and as it was now the 8th of July and very warm, Cartier called it the Bay of Chaleur (heat). Landing on the Gaspé peninsula, he carried off a couple of Indians, then crossed to Anticosti, where he was actually at the entrance of the opening he sought to the westward, had he only known it. But the summer was passing, and there was not enough food to supply his company much longer, so he sailed once more through the Straits of Belleisle, and was back at St. Malo by the 1st of September.

He set out again the next year with three ships and a mixed company, consisting of gentlemen rovers who wanted to go, criminals from the jails who did not want to go, and the two Indians kidnapped at Gaspé. Once more they reached the wonderful Bird Island, at the north of Newfoundland, and sailed through the Straits of Belleisle onwards to the passage between the island of Anticosti and the mainland. There they saw a lot of whales, and on the 10th of August—the festival of St. Lawrence—they entered a small bay to which was given the name that afterwards extended both to gulf and river.

The two captive Indians told Cartier that he was at the mouth of a mighty stream that flowed from *Kanata*, a Huron-Iroquois word, meaning village, but he would not believe them, though he kept on to the westward, in the hope that this time he had really found the sea passage through to the Indies. But the water began to get fresh and presently land on either side of the river could be seen. Near the mouth of the Saguenay were some natives in canoes who paddled off in terror at sight of the strangers, till the two Indians on board shouted to them to come back, which they did, and greeted the Frenchmen very gladly. Further on, past the island of Hazel-nuts, still called *Ile-aux-Coudres*, they met more savages, and among them the great chief Donnacona, who lived at Stadacona, an Indian town where Quebec now stands. Cartier's ships came to anchor at last beside a beautiful island which was covered with the vines of wild grapes; and therefore he called it the Isle of Bacchus, but now it is named Orleans. On September 14th a better anchorage was found at the mouth of the little river running into the St. Lawrence below the heights of Stadacona, and now called the St. Charles.

Cartier left some of his company there, but he was bound to sail further on up the great river with the rest, though the travelled Indians who had gone back to their friends were shy of coming near the ships again to act as guides. Donnacona, likewise, was none too sure of what these strangers meant to do in his country, and would rather have seen them turning back down the river than going farther on; but Cartier only laughed at the childish way the chief tried to frighten him out of his purpose—dressing Indians up as demons, and so on.

1535. It took the Frenchmen about two weeks to make the journey between what are now Quebec and Montreal, and it was the first week of October before they reached the site of the latter, where then stood the Indian town of Hochelaga. It consisted of about fifty wooden lodges, surrounded by a fence, or palisade, for defence, which had only one gate. Just above this entrance was a platform, or gallery, to which the warriors could climb up and throw down stones or shoot their arrows at an enemy trying to get in. The people were probably of the Huron-

Iroquois family, for they were not simply hunters but grew a little corn about their village, and they gave Cartier and his men some bread made out of it. Fish was also set before the strangers, who presented beads, knives, and hatchets in exchange.

The whole village went wild with delight over the bearded visitors clad in armour, and, looking upon their leader as a divine person, they brought him their sick to heal with his touch. At his request they led him by a steep path to the very top of the high wooded hill at the back of the town, and he called it Mount Royal. Jacques Cartier was the first of Europeans to look out upon that wide prospect of river, forest, and mountain, and the only one to see the Indian town of Hochelaga. Sixty-eight years afterwards, when the next visitors from France came to Mount Royal, village and people had both disappeared. The Iroquois could probably have told what had become of them.

Cartier and his companions stayed on the island for three days, and being quite convinced that no outlet through the continent was to be found in that direction, they returned to Stadacona, where Cartier resolved to spend the winter. He might have chosen a warmer place. Those travellers from the sunny land of France were not prepared to find, in a latitude lower than that of Paris, ice-bound rivers, keen, biting winds, and snowdrifts as high as their heads. They built a rude fort, at the mouth of the Lairet, a tiny stream running into the St. Charles. Soon the scurvy appeared, a loathsome disease caused by "exposure to a moist, cold, foul atmosphere, with long use of one kind of food and of stagnant water." All but ten of the men took it, and twenty-five had died before a friendly Indian told them how to make a drink from the spruce-tree that cured the remainder.

When the month of May came round, and the ice broke up in the great river, the survivors sighed to go home, so Cartier set up a cross with the arms of France upon it, as a sign that he had taken possession of the country for his king, and departed. So many of his men had died, he needed only two ships for the return trip, and he therefore destroyed the smallest, leaving it behind. Its remains were discovered in the river St. Charles, three hundred and seven years afterwards.

That Jacques Cartier was a bit of a pirate is seen from the fact that he coaxed the Indian chief, Donnacona, and nine of his principal men on board one of his vessels when he was ready to sail and would not let them go again, though the Indian people begged him to do so. They followed him in their canoes as far as the island of Hazel-nuts (Coudres), and were not satisfied till Donnacona himself came on deck and told them that he was all right and would be back again the next year. He never did come back, for he died in France, and so did all the rest of the kidnapped party, except one little girl.

1541. No wonder, then, that when Jacques Cartier returned to the river St. Lawrence upon his third voyage he did not find the savages so friendly as before. Indians do not forget. Cartier told them Donnacona was dead, and that news was pleasing to the chief who ruled in his stead, but of the other nine he said they were all married to Frenchwomen, and so happy and rich they had refused to return to their own country. The two Indians who had been to France were not likely to believe that story, and they stirred up their friends against the kidnappers, so that they thought it safer to go a little farther from Stadacona than the St. Charles, and they built another fort at Cap Rouge.

Cartier sailed up the St. Lawrence once more, and tried in vain to get farther west than Hochelaga. The rapids barred the way. Upon this voyage he was supposed to be acting under the orders of a nobleman called Roberval, whom King Francis was sending out with colonists to plant a settlement of which he would be governor. Jacques Cartier was not the kind of man who cared to take orders from another, and whether he did it purposely or not, certain it is that he had spent his second winter in Canada and had left for home again before Roberval and his settlers arrived.

The fort at Cap Rouge was there, however, and in a large house they built close by, the new-comers spent a wretched winter. Scurvy was not the only foe they had to fight. Most of the colonists were jail-birds, sent out against their will, who, instead of doing their best to begin a new life in a new country, quarrelled among themselves and were so bad in every way that Roberval had to punish them by lashing, imprisonment, and even by hanging. He, too, tried to explore the great river, but lost eight of his men in the attempt, and the news he sent back to France was so hopeless that Cartier was told to go and bring both colonists and governor home.

Nothing daunted that brave mariner. He came out in the autumn and spent a third winter in Canada, sailing home with Roberval and company in the spring. France was much taken up with her wars of religion with Spain, but when another breathing spell came she made another attempt to colonise Canada. Roberval and his brother were sent out with settlers, but the ship went down and all on board were lost.

1549. The voyages of Cartier had made it plain that a short cut to India was not to be found through the middle of America, but the brave sailors of that time still had hope of finding it to the northward. Martin Frobisher, in the reign of Queen Elizabeth, made three voyages with that object in view, and after him John Davis made three more, but no result followed except the naming of Frobisher's Bay and Davis Strait. Both men left it on record that a north-west passage to the Indies was possible, and thus they inspired the later band of gallant Arctic explorers. " I think it might be done, and England should do it," was the line Millais, the artist, wrote below his picture of an old sea captain, even in the nineteenth century.

1578. Sir Francis Drake, who sailed all round the world in Elizabeth's time, was one of the first visitors to the Pacific Coast of what is now called Canada. He went northward as far as Alaska, some say, but it was near San Francisco that he stayed on shore for five weeks and took possession of the whole coast for England.

1583. Sir Humphrey Gilbert did more. His was the first English attempt at founding a colony, and the place he chose was the island of Newfoundland. Ill-fortune met him from the first. So many men took sick in one of the ships that she had to turn back. Another was lost in an exploring trip from the island, and fearing famine for his colonists, Sir Humphrey decided to take them home to England. He himself was on board the *Squirrel*, a tiny craft of only ten tons burden, when it was lost in a storm. Some of his last words have come down to us—" Courage, my lads! Heaven is as near by sea as by land."

1592. A Greek pilot, called Juan de Fuca, was sent by the Spanish viceroy of Mexico to sail northward along the Pacific coast and see if he could not find a passage through to the Atlantic Ocean. He thought he had found it at the south of Vancouver Island, when he sailed into the wide channel which is now named after him; but his discovery was scoffed at by the sailors of his own and a later day, who declared that the Straits of Juan de Fuca did not exist.

NEW BRUNSWICK

PART SECOND

TO THE END OF THE SEVENTEENTH CENTURY

CHAPTER IV

THE ROMANCE OF ACADIA

HILE France was busy at home, in the war with Spain, fighting her own subjects also about their religion, she had no time to attend to Canada, and left it alone for half a century. So soon as there was peace within the borders of Old France, the Marquis de la Roche was made viceroy of New France, with power to control its trade, grant land to settlers, and, in short, to

have all things his own way ; but these wide powers proved to be of small use to him.

1598. As colonists he had to take prisoners from the jails, and his sailors too were mostly pressed into the service against their will. Being afraid that his settlers would desert if he landed on, or near, the mainland of America, the Marquis put them ashore on Sable Island, more than a hundred miles from the coast of Nova Scotia, to stay there until he found a place for them ; but his little ship was caught up in a gale from the west and driven straight back to France. There he found his enemies in power, and they had him put in prison, so that it was five years before he could get the ear of the king to tell him about the convicts he had left to their fate.

As if cold and hunger were not enough to fight, those wretched men had fallen to fighting one another, and when at last a ship was sent to rescue them from Sable Island, only twelve out of the forty were found alive. They had built a frail house for themselves out of an old wreck, and had lived by fishing and by hunting the descendants of the cattle Baron de Léry had left on the island. Henry the Fourth expressed a wish to see these long-bearded, fierce-looking men, dressed in the skins of wild animals, and when he heard their story he gave them fifty crowns apiece and a pardon for all their past sins; but the Marquis de la Roche was so much disappointed at the failure of his grand schemes for a colony that he pined away and died.

The next attempt to found a settlement in Canada was made at Tadousac, where the Saguenay River enters the St. Lawrence. Out of sixteen men who were left there to get valuable furs from the Indians in exchange for a few beads, knives, and hatchets, four died, and the rest would have shared their fate had not the natives taken pity on them, and when winter came, warmed and fed them in their wigwams.

Pontgravé was the name of the merchant who had thus tried to add to his riches by the fur trade, but upon his next voyage to the St. Lawrence for the same purpose, four years later, he had with him a man of a higher stamp. This was Captain Samuel de Champlain, of the Royal Navy, who had served as a soldier too, yet was like a priest in his piety, and zeal for converting the heathen.

1603. Pontgravé and Champlain crossed the ocean in two vessels so small that a man would be considered mad who would venture out upon the inland lakes in one of them, if the water were rough. Nevertheless, they arrived safely in the Gulf of St. Lawrence, and sailed up the broad river of the same name, past the present sites of Quebec and Montreal, where the Indian villages that Cartier had found there were no longer to be seen. But the rapids of St. Louis, near the island of Mount Royal, ran swiftly as ever, and as before they had prevented Cartier from going further up the river, they now prevented Champlain. He returned to France and did not go into the St. Lawrence upon his second voyage the next year. This was taken in company with a Huguenot nobleman, M. de Monts, who had got leave from the king to colonise Acadia, a tract of country in which were included the present Nova Scotia, New Brunswick, and part of the State of Maine.

De Monts was made viceroy of all that region ; and besides Champlain, there sailed with him the Baron de Poutrincourt, while Pontgravé followed later with supplies. They explored the Bay of Fundy and discovered the beautiful Annapolis Basin, with which Poutrincourt was so much delighted that De Monts made him a present of land upon its shores. After seeing that suitable site for a colony, why they should have fixed upon St. Croix, a barren little island at the mouth of the river of the same name, cannot be told. But there the settlers were landed—a mixture of nobles and convicts, Protestants and Catholics, soldiers and working men—eighty in all. A rude fort was built, as well as a chapel, a house for the viceroy, barracks and storehouses.

Poutrincourt went home to bring out another band of colonists for the settlement he intended to found at his new domain on Annapolis Basin which he called Port Royal. Pontgravé went off on a trading trip up the St. Lawrence, and thence back to France, but De Monts and Champlain spent the winter at St. Croix. A bitter cold one it turned out to be. The men fell ill of the scurvy, and nearly half of them died before Pontgravé came to their relief with supplies in the spring. Champlain alone had kept up his courage, and whenever the weather permitted he had sailed on exploring trips, visited different points along the coast, as far south as Cape Cod, and gone also some distance inland, which none before him had done. Being geographer to the king, he took notes of the natives and their customs, as well as of the plants and animals he saw; and he wrote them down in his diary with good literary style.

1605. Nowhere had either he or the viceroy seen a better place for a settlement than Poutrincourt's grant at Port Royal, so rather than spend another winter at St. Croix, the colony was moved over there in August. The buildings taken down on one side of the Bay of Fundy were set up on the other. Then De Monts and Poutrincourt went home to France on business while Pontgravé and Champlain were left in charge at Port Royal. The second winter was not nearly so hard as the first had been, and Champlain, as before, did his best to keep up the spirits of the colonists, but it was not easy to do that when the food began to run short.

Pontgravé feared that De Monts had forgotten his settlers, and he had actually embarked with all but two to seek help from some of the French fishing-boats likely to be found near the banks of Newfoundland, when M. de Poutrincourt sailed into the basin. Pontgravé and his shipload were not far off, and were soon recalled to make a fresh start at Port Royal.

The third winter was mild for Acadia, and the settlers had learned through their hard times how and what to hunt for food. They had made friends with the Micmac Indians of the neighbourhood, especially with an old chief, called Membertou, who brought a number of his people to set up their wigwams near Port Royal. They taught the French to trap the hare and the beaver, to follow the big moose on snowshoes far into the trackless woods, and in return they were made welcome to the fort and to the fare within, whatever it might be.

There were fish and game in plenty, and Champlain started a spirit of friendly rivalry among fifteen of his comrades to see which would provide the best fare for the table of Poutrincourt. These skilful sportsmen called themselves "The Order of the Good Time," and good times indeed seemed in store for the whole colony when it suddenly got a "Notice to Quit." The power granted to De Monts had been taken from him as carelessly as it had been given, and therefore the colony he had tried so hard to plant in Acadia had to be deserted just as the sun was beginning to shine upon it.

Such a thing as a settlement supporting itself, as those of New England did, was never dreamed of in New France. The Pilgrim Fathers came out to Plymouth of their own free will, to escape persecution for their religion at home, as the Huguenots of France would have been only too glad to do, had they been allowed. The first settlers of Canada were taken out by some rich nobleman, like De Monts, to whom the king had given a charter. When the Viceroy of Acadia could no longer keep up Port Royal, it was deserted, and the fields that had been cleared and planted were left to Membertou and his tribe.

While the French had thus been striving to keep a hold upon Acadia, English sailors were reaching into the heart of the northern regions. Henry Hudson had made three voyages to America and had left his name on a river of modern New York before he sailed through the straits called after him, into the vast bay which also bears his name. He spent the winter upon its shores, but his cowardly crew rose against him and set him adrift in an open boat along with his son and a few loyal sailors. They were never heard of again.

Always searching for a passage to the Pacific, English explorers kept on sailing into Hudson's Bay, in spite of the fate of its discoverer; but they did no more than christen unknown waters, such as Baffin's Bay and James Bay.

1610. The same year that Hudson was lost saw Poutrincourt back in Acadia. He was determined not to give up the land which had been granted to him, and which was his by right. It was three years before he could get the king to listen to his claim, but when at last he landed again in Port Royal with a shipload of settlers, he found the houses and furniture just as they had been left. The Indians had stolen nothing, and they were overjoyed to see the Frenchmen back again, especially the chief, Membertou, who was now over one hundred years old.

Poutrincourt had a brave young son, called Biencourt, eighteen years of age, whom he sent home to France to get help for the colony, but by that time Henry the Fourth was dead, and with him had died all interest in Acadia except among the Jesuit priests and a few of their wealthy converts. Beincourt came back and Poutrincourt went over, but in his absence a crushing blow fell on Port Royal.

1613. Captain Samuel Argall, of Virginia, sailing northward to the fishing banks of Newfoundland, was filled with patriotic wrath at hearing of the French settlement, for had not Cabot claimed the whole of the mainland for England before Verrazano took possession of it for France? The Virginians landed and utterly destroyed Port Royal. Biencourt was from home at the time, or they might not have had so easy a victory. With Charles de la Tour and a few remaining followers, he spent the winter in the woods, without a roof for shelter, and there his father, Poutrincourt, found him in the spring.

Argall's raid called the attention of England to Acadia, and King James the First resolved to settle some of his own countrymen in it.

1620. He granted the whole of Acadia to a Scotchman, Sir William Alexander, who brought colonists to the Port Royal Basin.

Poutrincourt died in 1615, but Biencourt had never given up his rights to the region, and at his death he left the property to his friend and comrade, Charles de la Tour. This brave young man made his headquarters near Cape Sable, at the place now named after him, while his father, Claude de la Tour, had a post on the Penobscot.

For awhile the Scotch and the French dwelt in peace, as Acadia was large enough for both, but presently war broke out between France and England, and Sir William Alexander thought the time had come to claim the whole country, and divide it among the proposed Order of Knights-Baronets of Nova Scotia, who would bring out settlers to their estates—when they got them.

To further this end, Sir William offered to include the La Tours, father and son, among the Knights-Barons, if they would peaceably give up their rights to the whole country, and be content with a portion. Claude de la Tour was well content to do this, for he had been to England as a prisoner, had married a wife there, and been well treated; so that he sailed with a load of colonists to occupy the estate promised to him and his son. They were both Huguenots, and could look for more kindness as English subjects than as French; but Charles de la Tour would not forsake his country. He held out in his Fort St. Louis, even against his own father, and Claude was obliged to take his settlers round to where the Scotch were already planted near Port Royal, which had been taken by the English.

1632. When peace came again, and the whole of Acadia was given back to France by the Treaty of St. Germain-en-Laye, Claude de la Tour had to seek safety with his son, who for his loyalty was made Lieutenant-General of Acadia. Other Frenchmen of high and low degree came out to lord it over the Scotch settlers, and to keep the English of Massachusetts at a proper distance; but Port Royal was deserted.

1643. The Seigneur d'Aulnay Charnisy, commander of a new Port Royal on the other side of the Basin from the old one, was very jealous of Charles de la Tour, to whom the king had granted land directly across the

Bay of Fundy, at the mouth of the river St. John, where he had better trade with the Indians of whom he was an old and tried friend. La Tour being a Protestant, there were many enemies ready to bear false witness against him when Charnisy sailed to France on purpose to gain his arrest. He got his desire—an order to take Charles across the sea to stand his trial—but the stouthearted La Tour refused to be taken, so Charnisy blockaded him in his fort and then lay in wait for a vessel with one hundred and forty emigrants and supplies that was coming from the Protestant city of Rochelle. When at length she appeared, Charles de la Tour and his wife managed to slip through the blockade in a rowboat, and got on board the Rochelle vessel, which took them off to Boston, and there they got help.

Charnisy never knew that his prey had escaped him till five ships from Boston appeared at his back and chased him across to his own side of the Bay of Fundy. Once more he tried to take the fort of La Tour when the master of it was away in Boston, and only the mistress left to defend it. This she did so bravely that Charnisy had to withdraw, very angry at being beaten by a woman for the second time. He had tried and failed to get her arrested for treason while she was in France clearing the good name of her husband.

Two months later, when Charles de la Tour was almost home with help from Boston, Charnisy came again to attack Madame de la Tour, and by this time the food was all done and her followers were in despair. She gave up the fight on the strength of the victor's promise to spare the brave men who had defended her husband's property and herself, but Charnisy basely broke his word and hanged them all. Madame was brought out, with a halter round her neck, to see them die, and Charnisy took her back to Port Royal with him, where she lived only three weeks.

1667. This bad man prospered for a time, but five years later he was drowned in a little river on his own estate, and who should marry his widow and fall heir to his command but Charles de la Tour? The King of France came to see that he was a much-wronged man, and made him governor of all Acadia. No sooner was he settled once more, and beginning to grow rich through the fur trade, than the country was taken by the English. La Tour went over to England, and laid before the Protector, Oliver Cromwell, the grants made to himself and his father by Sir William Alexander, and these were restored to him. He had to do the same when Charles the Second came to the throne, but finally the whole of Acadia was given back to France by the Treaty of Breda.

By this time the English had planted a settlement in Newfoundland, but it did not grow very fast because the rich fish merchants did not want people coming in, as they thought, to spoil their trade. The French came in, however, and by 1660 they had a strong post at Placentia, although they had only got leave from the English to land on the island for the purpose of drying fish.

NOVA SCOTIA

CHAPTER V

THE FATHER OF NEW FRANCE

AMUEL DE CHAMPLAIN was born at Brouage, on the Bay of Biscay, in 1567, and he was therefore thirty-six years of age when first he went sailing up the St. Lawrence with the merchant, Pontgravé. He had seen enough on that trip to make him long to explore the great river farther, and five years later, he set out again in the same company, this time to found the colony for De Monts which he had failed to place in Acadia.

1608. That it could be easily defended was a point always looked for in the planting of a new settlement, and Champlain was too good a soldier not to see how well a fort could command the great river if built on the high, steep bluff at a place called by the Indians "Quebec," meaning the narrows, or a strait. The three buildings that were first put up were so close together that they were more like one, and that one was a curious mixture of dwelling, storehouse, armory, and blacksmith's shop, called the "Habitation." It had a dove-cote too, and though entirely of wood, it tried to copy a feudal castle in moat and drawbridge. Beyond these was Champlain's garden, in which it was his great delight to see how the different seeds would come up that he brought with him from France.

The "Habitation of Quebec" must have stood near the present corner of Notre Dame and Sous le Fort Streets, not far from the Lower Town Market. A wooden wall was built about it on which were mounted three small cannon, that guarded it well enough, for as yet the Indians had no firearms. But its first foes were from within.

Some of the men who had come out to stay did not see why they should labour at felling trees, or at ploughing up the rather rocky soil, when it would be so much easier to make themselves rich at once through the fur trade, as others were doing. Had the commander been a weak man, his colony would have been strangled at its birth, but Champlain was both strong and wise. Getting wind of a plot, he hanged the maker of it, and when Pontgravé sailed in September with his load of furs, he sent other three of the worst plotters back to France with him, to be punished there.

Champlain was strong in body as in mind, so that he did not suffer from the scurvy, but twenty of his men died of it that first winter, and only eight were left alive when Pontgravé came back in the spring.

The Spaniards who first landed in North America killed the Indians as if they were wild animals; the English took no account of them, except where they stood in the way of white settlers, but the French always tried to make friends with them. That had been the rule in Acadia, and Champlain followed the same at Quebec, though very troublesome friends they often were. The nearest to him were the Montagnais of the Algonquin family, who had no settled homes, but moved their wigwams from place to place during the hunting season. They would eat up all their food at the beginning of the winter, so that they were generally starving towards the end, and would come begging to the " Habitation of Quebec," though the French there had often little enough for themselves.

To keep friends with these Indians, as well as those to the westward whose country he wanted to explore, Champlain found that he would have to take up their quarrel with the Iroquois, the noted Five Nations who lived to the south and west of him. He has been much blamed for doing this, but the war was not of his making. It had been going on for years, and he had to take one side or the other if he did not wish to make enemies of both. It seemed right to him to fight for his first friends, the Montaignais, and their allies, the Algonquins and Hurons of the west.

1609. About sixty of them met in the end of May at the mouth of the Richelieu, called at that time the "River of the Iroquois," because it flowed directly from their country into the St. Lawrence. Champlain and two other Frenchmen went with the war party in their canoes the whole length of the Richelieu and onward into the lovely lake which is still called after the first white man known to have seen it, Lake Champlain. They fell in with two hundred Iroquois near the modern Crown Point, and the fight was but short. The three Frenchmen went in front of their allies, and when the Iroquois saw their arrows glance off from the strangers' armour without hurting them in the least, and heard the terrible crack of their guns which brought down one of their own chiefs stone dead and wounded another and yet another, these bravest of all Indians took to their heels and ran off into the woods like a pack of frightened children, with the allies after them, killing and taking prisoners.

Next summer the Hurons and Algonquins begged "the man with the iron breast" to lead them once more against the Iroquois, and once more he agreed. This time they met the foe about three miles from the present town of Sorel, which stands at the mouth of the Richelieu. They had made a fence to hide themselves by cutting down trees and bushes, but Champlain and his Indians broke through it, and the hundred Iroquois, fighting bravely to the last, were all killed or drowned in the river, except fifteen who might well wish they had been killed too, instead of being kept alive for the torture.

The colony at Quebec could not yet keep itself, and De Monts, its supporter in the old land, was rapidly growing poor. He was no longer the only one who had the right to trade with the Indians, and the men who came for that purpose to Tadousac and Quebec merely wanted to make money and go away again. They did not care whether the country were ever settled or not. Champlain alone never sought riches for himself, but faithfully kept the trust committed to him, whether by one person or by many, and looked only to the prosperity of Canada.

For ten or twelve years he went to France every autumn and sailed back to Quebec every spring. These voyages in the small, badly-found ships of the time were by no means pleasure excursions, but Champlain was a man who never spared himself when duty called him, whether it was to seek from the great ones of France the desired aid for his colony or to visit the Indians in their wigwams and put up with their customs, in order to gain their help when he needed it.

1613. The dream that a way to China and the East might yet be found through North America was still common among Europeans, and Champlain, having faith in it, went on a long and hard canoe journey up the Ottawa River, so far as the island of Allumette, visiting the Indians there, who told him that there was no near outlet into a great northern sea, as he had been led to believe.

Two summers later he followed the same route again, but went on and on, with Indian guides, and passed into a branch of the

Ottawa called the Mattawan. From the head of that stream the two canoes were carried across to Lake Nipissing, thence paddled by way of the French River into Georgian Bay, the island-bordered wing of Lake Huron.

For two weeks Champlain stayed in the country of the Huron Indians and visited twenty of their villages. The people took it for granted that he had come to lead out their warriors against the Iroquois, and that is what he had to do, although those Indian wars, with their horrible cruelties to prisoners, were not much to his taste.

The journey was a long one through a part of the country new to white men, but now called the Province of Ontario. Since it was entirely covered by woods at that time, the Indians went by water wherever they could, and the war party left the Huron country by way of Lake Simcoe. Carrying their canoes through the forest, here and there, from one lake or stream to the next, they reached the Trent River, which brought them down to the wide, blue water of Lake Ontario. Champlain was the first white man who had seen it, and it was looking its best with the trees on its banks and islands decked out in their autumn colours, ruby and gold.

Crossing the lake at its eastern end, the party reached the southern shore not far from the present city of Oswego, and soon they were marching afoot, Indian file, that is, one behind another, along a narrow trail, into the country of the dreaded Iroquois. In their previous fights under Champlain, it had been the most eastern of the Five Nations, the Mohawks, they had attacked, but now they were bent on destroying a village of the Onondagas, the very centre of the union. The place was well fenced about, and the Hurons had not the patience to carry out their leader's plans for the taking of it, so they were defeated. Champlain himself being wounded, had to be carried off by his Indian friends, who were now in as great haste to get away from the fight as they had been to get into it. When they once more reached the shores of Lake Ontario, which Champlain was sure led into the St. Lawrence, then called "the great river of Canada," he begged for a guide and a canoe to take him back directly to his own countrymen, but the Hurons were in too great fear of the Iroquois to venture that way, and told him he must return as he had come, by the French River and the Ottawa.

It was now the month of October, and by the time the war party had got back to the Huron country, they declared it was too late in the season for Champlain to go to his friends by the northern route, and that he must spend the winter with them. This he did, making the best of his time by learning more about the people of that part of the country, their customs, and their language. When at length he took the roundabout way back again in the spring, the people in Quebec wept for joy at seeing him once more, for they had all believed him dead.

1617. The first family which settled in Quebec was that of a man called Hébert. He came up from Acadia, where he had been with Biencourt, and brought his two daughters, who were married shortly afterwards. Hébert and his sons-in-law were the first to grow grain and vegetables on the ground of Quebec, and when times of famine came, as they often did, they could have sold their little produce ten times over.

1620. Madame Champlain lived with her husband in the colony for four years, and though but a girl of twenty when she came out, did her best to teach the Indian squaws and their children, but the work was too hard for her, and the climate too harsh. She returned to France, and after her husband's death, having no children, she became an Ursuline nun. The only memento of her left in Canada is Ste. Helen's Isle, near Montreal, which her husband had named after her the year of their marriage, 1611. He had noticed that island with the eye of a soldier, as being a good place for a defence, just as he had remarked the importance of having a trading post on the island of Montreal, and had gone so far as to choose the site for a settlement, near where the Custom House is now.

Though he had been two winters in Acadia and one in the Huron country, that of 1620-21 was but the second Champlain had passed in Quebec, and he employed himself building a fort to protect it better. This was set up on the cliff behind the "Habitation," on part of the ground that is now covered by Dufferin Terrace, the favourite promenade of Quebec people on summer evenings.

The governor had worries in plenty besides the keeping of a foothold at all on the rock of Quebec. None but a man of very good judgment, as well as good nature, could have got on so well with the mixed lot he had under him. He needed plenty of tact for his dealings both with white men and red, with Catholics and Huguenots, and he was respected by all as a man who had a humble opinion of himself, but a high one of his country and the credit that Canada ought to be to her.

It was a crushing blow to his hopes when

war broke out between France and England, and the ships of the enemy were reported at Tadousac on their way up to take Quebec. Soon enough they appeared, and Admiral Kirke called upon Champlain to surrender; but the brave Frenchman replied, "We will fight to the last!" and the Englishman did not know how little he had to fight upon. Quebec looked like a place not to be easily taken, so Kirke sailed off down the river again to try if he could not meet and capture the supply ships coming out from France, and thus starve out the people below the rock. That is what he succeeded in doing, but it took him some time to dispose of the whole eighteen vessels laden with colonists, arms, and provisions for Quebec, and therefore it was the next year before he came back to complete his conquest.

1629. Things were in even worse shape by that time, and Champlain could do naught but surrender. Kirke was a very gentlemanly conqueror, and he treated well both the people who stayed in Quebec and those he brought off to England. Champlain was among the latter, and he was a prisoner on parole in London for about a month before he was allowed to return to France.

He had worked too hard and too long for Canada not to regret its loss, but there were many of his countrymen who thought it a good riddance. The cost of the colony had outweighed any good it had done to the mother country, and to defend it against the Iroquois, as well as against the English settlers that were rapidly filling up the seaboard of the Atlantic, would take more men and money than it was considered worth to keep a handful of colonists on the St. Lawrence. When taken by Admiral Kirke there were only five families in Quebec, and a total of less than one hundred souls. The houses of the colony were all built of logs, excepting a single stone one at Tadousac. There was another trading-post at Three Rivers, between Quebec and the island of Montreal, and at Cap Tourmente were a few sheds for sheltering cattle.

1632. Nor did England greatly prize her new possession, though her people were by no means pleased when it was given back to France at the declaration of peace. The next summer Champlain was once more sent out as governor.

1635. He was now a man of sixty-six, and might have looked for ease in his old age, but he took none, and, like the high-minded, honourable gentleman that he was, he laboured to the last for the good of others. He died at Quebec on Christmas Day in the Fort of St. Louis, which he had set upon the cliff, and he was buried close to the church he had built in honour of the recovery of the colony.

A pious man of pure life, Champlain was mourned long in the colony of which he had been the heart and soul, but five years after his death the church of Notre Dame de la Recouvrance was burned, and his burial-place was lost sight of for centuries. In 1856, some men who were laying water-pipes discovered a mouldering coffin and a few bones in a lofty vault on the hillside in Little Champlain Street, at the foot of Breakneck Stairs. It seemed as if a person of some consequence had been buried there, and that person is supposed to have been Samuel de Champlain, the Father of New France.

BRITISH COLUMBIA

CHAPTER VI

THE MISSIONARIES

THE earliest visitors to America had nearly always a priest on board their vessels, for the clergy of the Roman Catholic Church never hesitated to risk their lives nor to endure great hardships in the hope of saving souls. From the first attempts at colonising by Spain, France, or Portugal, the conversion of the Indians was thought to be of first importance, and this was specially true in Canada.

De Monts being a Huguenot, it was ministers of his own faith he took with him to Acadia, but he agreed that the teaching of the natives should be left to the priests. To this end Poutrincourt, a liberal Roman Catholic, brought one out when he returned to make his second attempt at the settlement of Port Royal in 1610. Membertou, the aged chief of the Micmacs, and a number of his followers, became Christians, and wanted to scalp those of their own tribe who would not likewise be baptised. But even this proof of conversion did not satisfy a certain wealthy and pious widow in France, who was as anxious to send out Jesuit missionaries as they were to come; and come they did, for the lady raised the funds, and it was she who became mistress of Acadia when Poutrincourt lost all his money. He disliked the Jesuits, who were noted for meddling in other affairs than those of religion. "Show me my path to heaven," he cried to one of them, "I will show you yours on earth."

But the Jesuits would not be governed by Poutrincourt, nor by his son, Biencourt, and much trouble arose, which ended in the priests making a settlement of their own at Mount Desert, an island so named by Champlain, off the coast of Maine. That settlement was afterwards destroyed by Argall, the Virginian sailor, who took Port Royal later in the same summer (1613).

1615. The next priests that came to Canada were of the Franciscan order, who, unlike the Jesuits, take a vow always to be poor, and, therefore, have not so much interest in the affairs of this world. These four Récollet friars, dressed in coarse gray gowns, with pointed hoods to pull over their heads, and sandals on their bare feet, came out with Champlain on one of his annual voyages. So eager was one of them—Le Caron—to be about his chosen work, he did not wait to help the others build a monastery at Quebec, but went before the governor on that notable journey to the country of the Hurons. He writes of his trip up the Ottawa, which must have seemed strange indeed to a friar just from France:—

"It would be hard to tell you how tired I was with paddling all day, with all my strength, among the Indians; wading the rivers a hundred times and more, through the mud and over sharp rocks that cut my feet; carrying the canoe and luggage through the woods to avoid the rapids and frightful cataracts, and half-starved all the while."

Le Caron made a hut of bark for himself near Thunder Bay, there set up his altar, and began to study the Huron language—not an easy task, for there was no European tongue the least like it. To gain interpreters the French would send Indians to France, or their own young men to winter among the savages. One of the latter, called Jean Nicolet, who spent many years among the native tribes, was the first white man known to have seen Lake Michigan, as Father le Caron was the first to reach Lake Huron. Nicholas Viel, who succeeded him in his mission, and who finished the dictionary of the Huron tongue Le Caron had begun, was drowned by his Indian guide in the rapids near Montreal, which are called Sault au Récollet to this day.

Another of the gray friars went off on a mission to the Montagnais, more difficult to work with than the Hurons because they had no settled homes, and still another, de la Roche Dallion, visited the Neutrals, near the Niagara River. Within ten years the Récollets had five missions in Canada—at Tadousac, Quebec, Three Rivers, Lake Nipissing, and among the Hurons. The field was too large for them, and they asked that Jesuits might be set out to help.

1625. Of the three who first accepted the invitation, Father Masse had already endured much hardship with the Micmacs of Acadia, Jean de Brébeuf, large and strong, looked as if he could stand anything, but Lalemant was of a more delicate built. Other Jesuits came later, and in a few years none but priests of their order were to be found in Canada, for, when a fresh start was made after the English had been in Quebec, the Récollets were forbidden to return.

1636. New France was now the property of a fur company called the Hundred Associates, and it was they who sent out a successor to Champlain in the person of a pious nobleman called Montmagny, who was governor of Canada for eleven years. During that time the power of the Jesuits grew very much, both in worldly matters and those of religion. Indeed for thirty years they were the real masters of Quebec; but their chief glory rests in their missions to the Hurons.

Before these could be established the priests had to live among the Indians, enduring, as best they might, the smoke and dirt of dwellings, where dogs and fleas and children had equal liberty. It may have been the necessity for keeping the peace in lodges, where so many families were gathered under one roof, that taught the red men how to hold their tongues. When a man wished to speak he was listened to with attention and never interrupted, no matter how tedious he might become; and this habit misled the missionaries very often. The Indians would agree to everything they were told, whether they believed it or not, that being their idea of politeness, and it was therefore hard to tell if they were really converted.

When they met the French in council it was wonderful what dignity they could assume. They thought it was weak and unworthy of a warrior to show any sign of feeling, even when being tortured to a frightful degree. If a prisoner could endure having his finger-nails torn off, the soles of his feet burned, his flesh cut in strips, his tongue and his eyes gouged out, without uttering a groan, he would be called a hero, and his enemies would drink his blood or eat his heart, in order that they might be made as brave.

The Indians did not eat one another, except in the case of extreme famine, but it was a part of their religion to feast on the flesh of their foes. This was one of the ideas the priests had to fight against, and another was the notion that dreams were sent to foretell events and to guide conduct. It was this belief that gave so much power to the champion dreamers, or "medicine men," the worst enemies of the Jesuits. Those conjurers told the people that the "black robes" had brought the small-pox and were the cause of every bit of ill-fortune that came to the tribe.

Over and over again the missionaries were in danger of losing their lives, but the harder the task the more energy they brought to it, and though their conversions were often no more than the baptism of dying infants, they constantly risked their lives in doing even so much. Their bravery and patience at last won the Hurons to look upon them as friends, and in about ten years there were half a dozen missions, named after as many different saints, established in the country between Lake Simcoe and Georgian Bay.

The Jesuits have left to the world what are called their Relations, or reports sent home to the head of their order, and upon these all Canadian historians have relied for an account of the events of this period. They are well written by scholarly men, notably Father le Jeune, who describes minutely his winter travels with a wandering band of Montagnais hunters on the Lower St. Lawrence, and the cold and famine from which he suffered in their company. When the Relations were published in France a great interest in missions was aroused, especially among wealthy ladies, like Madame de la Peltrie, who determined to found a school for Indian girls at Quebec. She carried out her scheme, and the nun she chose for Lady Superior was Marie de l'Incarnation, a tall, strong woman, forty years of age, with a good head for business ; no mere dreamer, though she had visions in plenty.

1639. Two other Ursulines and three hospital nuns came out on the same ship, and the Ursuline Convent and the Hôtel Dieu were founded. The latter was first placed at Sillery, three miles above Quebec, where there was a mission to the Algonquins, but fear of the Iroquois caused its removal nearer the fort. The Ursulines made their first building of stone, and part of it still stands in the Upper Town.

Madame de la Peltrie was a lady with a love of variety, and she next joined an expedition to the island of Montreal to establish a religious settlement there. This was under the leadership of a devout soldier, called Maisonneuve, who came from France with forty men and four women. He was not to be turned from his purpose by the advice of Governor Montmagny, who thought it extremely rash for so small a company to place themselves in the very track of the Iroquois, and who recommended the island of Orleans instead.

1641. "It is my duty and my honour to found a colony at Montreal," said Maisonneuve, "and I would go if every tree were an Iroquois"—which every tree shortly became. An Algonquin, chased by those terrible hunters of men, ran for safety to the new French fort below Mount Royal, and thus showed the Iroquois where it was. They had now got firearms from the more reckless of the fur traders as well as from the Dutch at Albany, and for twenty years and more Canada writhed under their attacks. They would prowl about a lonely settlement and lie in wait for hours or days at a time in order to cut off a solitary tiller of the soil. Two or three men had to work close together in a field, for numbers alone would keep off the Iroquois.

Instead of soldiers, Maisonneuve had nuns to protect his tiny town, Ville-Marie de Montréal. The hospital stood without the walls of the fort, but it had a palisade of its own, and being built of stone was a solid little fortress in itself. Mademoiselle Mance was the head, and she and her nuns laboured long for the cure of the Indians, both body and soul. They gathered every year at Montreal in great numbers to sell their furs to the traders, but the Iroquois were ever on the watch to cut them off on their way down from the west.

Champlain had hoped to unite the whole of the Algonquin family to the Hurons, and if he had succeeded and the French had kept control of the league, which would have been the largest and strongest on the continent, they need no longer have feared the Iroquois. But the Algonquins were not strong-minded enough to make good links of a chain, and neither were the Hurons. The latter were as brave and more amiable than the Iroquois, but not so clever. The influence of the Jesuits was all towards peace, but that did not prevent the Iroquois from making war upon their converts. In 1648-49, one Huron village after another was destroyed and its people slain or carried off to be adopted into the tribes of their conquerors. The Jesuits did not escape. Brébeuf and Lalemant were put to death with frightful tortures, and Daniel also was killed.

The remnant of Hurons and their remaining priests took refuge upon Christian Island at the southern end of Georgian Bay, in the hope that the Iroquois might not find them there ; but fear and famine soon proved too strong for the refugees. Some of them scattered in small bands farther west, some openly asked for adoption into the tribes of the Senecas and got it ; while the rest were led by the priests to the island of Orleans.

Even there they were not safe. In 1656, the Iroquois made a raid and carried off a number of prisoners, making them dance and sing in scorn as they passed below the guns of Quebec. Those that were left fled into the town itself and stayed there for ten years, till the danger was over, when they were sent out to the village of Ste. Foye and thence to Lorette, where their descendants, mixed in blood with the French, remain to the present day.

The Huron captives among the Iroquois always welcomed the Jesuits as their friends, and whenever the Iroquois wanted peace, or pretended to want it, they would come to Quebec and demand that a missionary be sent to live among them. The Jesuits might well have refused to go, but none of them ever did, though death by torture was what they might expect. Father Jogues, the first white man to see Lake George, lived through frightful tortures, and gave thanks that he was permitted to teach the Iroquois. Once he made his escape, but went back to them again, and that time he was murdered by the Mohawks. The Onondagas also wanted a missionary, who had at length to use fraud to save the lives of himself and the Frenchmen with him. They invited the Indians to one of the great feasts at which it was correct to eat up all that was presented, and when the guests were helpless with overfeeding, the Frenchmen made their escape into Lake Ontario in some boats they had built in secret for the purpose. Others, elsewhere, were not so fortunate. Eight at least of the Jesuit missionaries were killed by the Indians ; one was frozen to death in the snow, and scarcely one escaped the torture.

1660. Montreal, Quebec and Three Rivers were trembling for their safety when Adam Daulac, Sieur des Ormeaux, commonly called Dollard, came to the rescue. He led out a small band of young men like himself from Montreal to lie in wait for a large war party of Iroquois which was coming down the Ottawa. The Frenchmen posted themselves at the foot of one of the rapids on that river, and though deserted by their Huron and Algonquin allies, they held out for eight days against fearful odds, till not one man was left alive to tell the tale. It was useless slaughter, one might say, but the Iroquois were discouraged from coming against Montreal at that time and the whole colony was saved.

PRINCE EDWARD ISLAND

CHAPTER VII

A ROYAL PROVINCE

WHILE the terrible Iroquois were on the war-path against the very existence of New France, one would imagine that her chief men would join together to protect her, and would think of nothing else ; but such was far from being the case.

1659. When the Jesuit rulers of Canada thought it time for her to have a bishop, they were determined that a man should be sent out for the office who would uphold their power ; and they got exactly what they wanted in M. de Laval. He was very clever, but narrow in his ideas, and set on having his own way ; for, as head of the church, he thought he could do no wrong. He would travel long distances in a canoe or on snowshoes, deny himself every luxury, sleep on a hard bed, eat food that others would not taste, and wait upon dirty poor people to show his holiness and humility. As a person, there was nothing too low for him ; but as a bishop there was nothing too high. He quarrelled with every governor who was sent out during his time on such points as— which should have the chief seat in church or at table ; which should be bowed to first on state occasions. The question really was—Is the bishop above the governor, the religious above the civil power, the church above the state?

Laval and the Jesuits answered "Yes," but the Vicomte d'Argenson, who had governed Canada for a year before Laval came out, answered "No." He was just as anxious to do his duty to the king as the bishop was to do his duty to the church ; and neither would give way to the other.

After Montmagny, the governors were sent out for three years only. They came and went, but Laval stayed on and grew in power and influence. He had lands given to him and gained riches, which he used for the good of the colony. He started a school at Cap Tourmente where youths might learn trades, and established two seminaries in Quebec; a preparatory one for boys, the other for the education of priests; and from these sprang Laval University (1852).

A standing subject of dispute between governor and bishop was the sale of brandy to the Indians. Laval preached against it, and threatened to put the sellers out of the church, which was the punishment most feared by good Catholics. The matter was hard to arrange, because the Indians had become very fond of strong liquors. If they did not get them from the French they would carry all their furs to the Dutch and English, and that would ruin Canada. There was not enough of her soil under cultivation to keep the people, and the fur trade was their main support. It was certainly necessary to control the sale of brandy, because the Indians could not control themselves in the drinking of it; but no half-way measures would do for Laval. The punishments for selling liquor grew more and more severe, and more and more young men turned *coureurs de bois.*

These runners of the woods, or what the English called bushrangers, often became as skilful hunters as the Indians themselves, dressing and fighting after their manner, even to the taking of scalps. It was not the lowest class in the country, but the highest who were most in love with the free life of the woods, which was much more to their taste than staying in Quebec, where they were punished for not going to mass and had to submit to strict rules of many kinds. Their fathers were generally poor, for the land system of Canada, unlike that of older countries, was more favourable to the tenant than to the owner. The seigneur, or lord of the soil, had to do more for the habitants on his estate than they did for him. To be sure, they had to fight for him; but his battles were theirs—against the Indians—and they paid him only a few cents an acre in rent, while he had to build a mill to grind their corn for them and also to serve as a fortress in time of need. M. Giffard of Beauport was the first seigneur in Canada not belonging to one or other of the religious bodies which were the chief landowners.

Another of Laval's troubles was the opposition of Montreal. The order of priests in power there was the Sulpician, whose members had no love for him nor the Jesuits, and around their seminary had grown up a hardy lot of colonists who were noted

Indian fighters and not so much inclined, as the people further down the river, to obey the church blindly in everything.

1661. The governor that came after d'Argenson was the Baron d'Avaugour, a bluff, honest old soldier, who had small patience with the bishop's desire to rule, and therefore Laval, through his powerful friends in France, not only had him removed before his term was up, but managed to get his choice of a successor over whom he thought to have complete control; but in this he was disappointed. Governor Mézy opposed the bishop and the Jesuits just as forcibly as the two before him had done; but the church party were too strong for him. He, too, was recalled at their request, but he died in harness.

1663. On the 5th of February there was an earthquake, which frightened the Canadians very much indeed and was looked upon as a judgment on the brandy-sellers. Walls and chimneys fell down; the ice in the river, three or four feet thick, was broken up, and smoke and clouds of sand flew out from the water. Hills were thrown into the St. Lawrence, to make islands there; and the jumbled-up look of the north shore about Les Eboulements marks the effect of that big earthquake, though there have been many smaller ones felt in the same region since.

The councillors appointed by Laval grew rich though the people stayed poor and did not grow in numbers; for while the lords of church and state squabbled, the lords of the forest stalked forth and scalped or carried off as prisoners whom they would.

This state of things made a deep impression on the mind of the King of France, Louis XIV., who was young and full of energy. He made up his mind to do what should have been done in Champlain's time, to turn New France into a royal province and manage its affairs himself. His first act was to send out one hundred families, a more hopeful kind of colonist than the single men whom love of adventure or the pursuit of wealth had brought hitherto. The king thus increased by five hundred the population of twenty-five hundred, of whom eight hundred were in Quebec.

1665. His next step was to make the Marquis de Tracy viceroy of all his American possessions, with the duty of adjusting affairs in Canada; and as a means to that end the king sent out with him the famous regiment of Carignan-Salières, twelve hundred hardened soldiers who were not likely to run away from any number of

Iroquois. The western nations of the Five were at peace with the French at that time, because they had their hands full in a war with the Eries, a family of Indians living near the lake named from them. The Mohawks, however, the nation of the Iroquois farthest east, took no part in the Erie war, but kept up their raids upon New France, by way of Lake Champlain and the Richelieu River, in spite of the three forts that had been put up in the hope of stopping them.

1666. M. de Tracy knew that they must be punished, and he set out for that purpose in the month of October with six hundred regular soldiers, six hundred Canadians, and a hundred Indians. The expedition went the same way that Champlain had gone more than fifty years before—through the lake called after him into the no less lovely one now named Lake George; thence by a long and difficult land and water journey of a hundred miles into the Iroquois country. The men were half-starved and quite worn out by the time they came to the first village of the Mohawks; but, happily, there was no fighting to be done, for the Indians had got word of their coming and had fled in dismay at the size of the army. They ran from the second village to the third, and on to the fourth and the fifth, all of which were burned by Tracy's men after they had taken as much food as they needed. Left without homes or provisions for the winter, the Mohawks were glad to make peace with the French, and Canada had little trouble with them for nearly twenty years.

The Marquis de Tracy left some of his soldiers behind him as colonists, but sailed for home with the rest; while M. de Courcelle stayed as governor, and M. Talon as intendant. The former, a soldier, was at the head of military matters; the latter, a lawyer, attended to business affairs. The one kept up the honour and glory of the king; the other acted as his private agent and looked after his money interests.

In truth the Canadians of old were a much-governed people, and would have got on far better if they had been left more to themselves, as the New Englanders were. Merchants were not allowed to bring over from France the goods they needed for trading with the Indians, but had to get them from a new company to whom the king gave the sole right to trade for forty years. During that time none but the company's vessels could take either freight or passengers to or from Canada.

Rules of that sort were enough to keep the people from striking out for themselves in any direction ; but Intendant Talon worked very hard to instruct them in the working of metals, the spinning of their own yarn, the weaving of their own cloth, and the making of their own caps and shoes. He visited the different *côtes*—a Canadian name for the homes strung along the banks of the St. Lawrence and the Richelieu. Each little village consisted of farmhouses facing the river, as the natural highway, and built close together for protection against cold and Indians, while the farms stretched for miles back into the country. The opening up of roads, the encouragement of porpoise fisheries, the giving of charity from the king—these were but a few of Talon's labours. The colonists were too well cared for to learn independence. Not only did the intendant import cows, sheep, and horses, he undertook to bring out wives for the settlers, chosen, as far as possible, from hardy country girls in France. About twelve hundred of them arrived within five years, and were married thirty at a time. Woe betide the luckless bachelor who refused to take a chance in the lottery! He was fined, forbidden to trade with the Indians, or to go into the woods for any purpose, and made so uncomfortable generally that, as a rule, he was glad enough to go to the appointed place within a fortnight after the ship's arrival to pick out a bride for himself.

The Sulpician, Father Dollier de Casson, wrote a history of Montreal which takes the place of a Jesuit Relation. A very large, strong man, full of good-humour, Dollier had been a soldier before he was a priest and never quite forgot his old calling. He was a prominent figure on Tracy's expedition against the Iroquois. His order became seigneurs of Montreal, and in the division of their lands they gave a large free grant at Lachine to Robert Cavelier, Sieur de la Salle, a young man of twenty-three just out from France, whose duty it then became to bring settlers who would clear the ground of trees and build a village of farmhouses, surrounded by a wooden fence or palisade, for a defence against Indians. Lachine was directly in the track of the tribes friendly to the French, coming down from the west with their furs; but it was also in the track of the Iroquois, coming more often in war than in peace.

La Salle, however, always got on well with all sorts of Indians, and had no trouble in learning their languages. A party of the Seneca nation spent a whole winter on his seigneurie and told him much about the

Ohio, "the beautiful river," that started in their country and became a wide and winding stream, flowing, La Salle imagined, into the Gulf of California. With a great mind and an enterprising spirit, he was not likely to confine himself long to the narrow limits of Lachine and the fur trade; but he was poor, and before he could set out on his longed-for expedition he had to sell his property back to the Sulpicians.

1669. When the head of the Montreal Seminary came in this way to hear of his plans it was decided to send a couple of Sulpician priests along with La Salle, so that the Jesuits might not have all the glory of converting the Indians of the west; and the chosen two were Fathers Galinée and Dollier de Casson. The party of twenty-four men in seven canoes, with Seneca guides, set out on the 6th of July, and by paddling and portaging up the St. Lawrence, reached Lake Ontario on the 2nd of August. Paddling the whole length of the big lake, they met, in a village of the Neutral Indians near the head of it, Louis Joliet, a Quebec merchant, on his way back from Lake Superior, where Talon had sent him to inspect the copper mines. The Sulpicians were so much pleased with Joliet's map of the route he had followed, from

Lake Erie, by way of the Grand River, they decided to go that way, but La Salle's mind was set upon the Ohio, and he was never the man to be turned from his purpose.

Therefore the party divided, the priests reaching Lake Erie and spending the winter near Long Point. In the spring they passed into Lake Huron and paddled away up to Sault Ste. Marie, where the Jesuit missionaries were not very glad to see them, so they only stayed three days and returned to Montreal by the French River and the Ottawa. The sole result of their long journey was a map which Father Galinée drew, very exact as to the parts visited, but wrong in making Huron and Michigan all one lake. La Salle corrected that error by coasting the shores of Lake Michigan the following year, when he also discovered the Illinois River. After the priests left him, he actually had reached the Ohio with the help of some Onondaga Indians, and had followed it down to the falls at Louisville.

1670. The Sulpicians were one means of lessening the power of the Jesuits, and Talon added another when he got leave for the Récollets to come back to Canada. They took up their old quarters at the convent on the St. Charles, and were as popular as before with the colonists; but for living among the Indians and keeping them loyal to the French they were not so useful as the Jesuits.

Nor did Talon confine his schemes for the good of Canada to the neighbourhood of Quebec and Montreal. He and Governor Courcelle were at one in their desire to extend the boundaries of New France far to the west and south, so that the English settlers might be confined to the Atlantic seaboard. With this view, though opposed to the lawless *coureurs de bois*, they encouraged respectable explorers, of whom the Jesuits were the most persevering.

1672. Charles Albanel, a priest of that order, was the first white man to reach Hudson's Bay by the overland journey from the head waters of the Saguenay, and he took possession of the whole region for the French king. Two years before that, it had been granted by the English king, Charles II., to his cousin, Prince Rupert, and about twenty lords and citizens calling themselves the Hudson's Bay Company.

After being driven by the Iroquois out of the Huron country, some of the Jesuits had gone west with their converts, and as early as 1660 they had made a map of Lake

Superior. Father Marquette was in charge of the mission to a remnant of the Hurons at Michilimackinac, the straits between Lakes Huron and Michigan, but, like most of his kind, his zeal was now divided between making conversions and making discoveries. He had been present at the gathering of Indians brought together at Sault Ste. Marie, the entrance of Lake Superior, by the famous explorer, Nicholas Perrot ; and he, like La Salle, had heard of the great river called by the natives, "The Father of Waters." He resolved to find it, if he could.

1673. With Louis Joliet and five other men in two canoes, Marquette started from his mission on the 17th of May. The party worked their way up the Fox River, already explored by Father Allouez of the Jesuit mission at Green Bay, and from the head of the stream, led by two Indian guides, they carried their canoes for more than a mile to the Wisconsin. Paddling down that river, they reached, on the 17th of June, the Father of Waters, the Mississippi, that they sought. They sailed down it as far as the mouth of the Arkansas, and then made the return journey by way of the Illinois to Lake Michigan, upon whose shores, two years later, Father Marquette found a lonely grave.

ONTARIO

CHAPTER VIII

FRONTENAC AND LA SALLE

IT was after the failure of his attempt to find a way to China by means of the great river he sought, that La Salle's late seigneurie on the island of Montreal came in scorn to be called Lachine; but he was not the man to give up. When one plan failed, he quickly made another. If the Mississippi, or the Ohio, which he thought the main stream, had no outlet into the Pacific Ocean, it must flow into the Gulf of Mexico. The Spaniards were strong in the south, but if the French could place a fort here and there along the banks of the great river and another at its mouth, a magnificent domain for their king might be built up in a climate milder than that of Canada. He thought, too, of the magnificent trade in furs that would include the skins of the bison, usually called the buffalo, which then roamed the western prairies in countless herds.

1672. The new governor, Count Frontenac, was just the man to see both the patriotic and the profitable sides of the question as La Salle saw them. He, too, was poor, and as he was fifty-two years of age he had less time to get rich than La Salle who was still under thirty. The first step they took together was the building of the fort, planned by Courcelle, at the eastern end of Lake Ontario, where the artillery barracks of the City of Kingston now stands. Frontenac went there in person with a goodly show of followers in order to impress the Iroquois whom he had told to meet him.

He was the first governor of Canada who was able to control those Indians, and he actually seemed to like them, as they did him. Indeed in character Frontenac was a bit of an Iroquois himself. He had all the fierce, unbending pride of one; was brave as their bravest, and cared almost as little for the suffering he caused. Other governors in trying to be friends with the Iroquois had called them "Brothers"; they let Frontenac address them as "Children," and scold them, as if they were really his children, when they did not do as he wished. He ruled them by fear, as well as by love, and kept his word to them, both about their presents and their punishments. Duchesneau, the intendant who came out after Talon, sided with Laval and the Jesuits, who hated Frontenac because he would in no way bend to their will, and even chose Récollets for his advisers in religion. They hated La Salle, too, and did not want him to go exploring in the west, because they intended that field should be kept for the Jesuits; but La Salle went in spite of them.

1678. He sailed from his post at Frontenac, on Lake Ontario, as far as the Humber River, near the present site of Toronto, and then across to the mouth of the Niagara, a winter voyage made with great difficulty; but La Salle was a man who spared neither himself nor those under him. Being very strong, both in mind and body, he expected too much of others, and that may have been the reason why, from white men at least, he gained more hate than love.

Father Hennepin who was on this expedition has left us the first description of the Falls of Niagara, though he exaggerates their height. There was also with La Salle his best friend and supporter, Henri de Tonty, an Italian by birth, who had lost a hand in battle before he came to Canada and had a steel one instead, with which he could give the Indians most astonishing blows in a fight.

1679. After setting up a storehouse for furs, near the Niagara's mouth, the party went on above the Falls and there built a vessel, which would carry forty-five tons, called the *Griffin*. She was the first to set sail upon Lake Erie, and it was in the month of August that she started, going on and on, through the Detroit River, up Lake Huron and down Lake Michigan till the head of Green Bay was reached. La Salle decided to send the *Griffin* back from there to Niagara with a load of furs to pay his debts. He never saw her again. Whether she was lost in the big storm that came up, or whether the pilot in charge stole the furs and sank her, La Salle never found out.

Meanwhile, unheeding cold and hunger, he and his men pushed on, by way of the St. Joseph and Kanakee Rivers, into the country of the Illinois Indians, from whom a branch of the Mississippi was named, and they built a fort upon it, called Crévecœur. There Tonty was left in charge, while La Salle went back to Frontenac for supplies, walking and paddling by turns fifteen hundred miles, through swamps, half-melted snow and drifting ice ; but his labour was in vain, for when he got back to his fort on the Illinois he found it in ruins. The men he left with Tonty had rebelled so soon as his back was turned, and had stolen all they could, while the Iroquois, on the war-path against the Illinois, had completed the destruction.

Father Hennepin, whom La Salle had sent with a couple of laymen to explore the Mississippi above the mouth of the Illinois, was taken prisoner by the Sioux Indians, and had many strange adventures before he was rescued by Du Lhut, the most famous *coureur de bois* of the time, who was said to be a partner of Frontenac in the fur trade.

Tonty and his few faithful followers made their way back to Green Bay, but La Salle did not find them till the next year, 1682, when they all once more set out for the Illinois, reached the Mississippi in canoes on February 6th, and followed its windings for two long months till the open water of the Gulf of Mexico was reached. Upon its shores La Salle set up a cross, taking possession of the whole country watered by the Mississippi and its tributaries in the name of the King of France, and calling it after him, Louisiana.

Returning to the Illinois, La Salle and Tonty chose a new site for a fort—a high rock on the river bank that could be easily defended—and upon the lowlands round about them settled hundreds of the Illinois, the Miamis, and other tribes of the Algonquin family who looked to the Frenchmen for protection against their common foe, the Iroquois. To keep control of these Indians and of the whole west, it was necessary to have goods for trade; but when he went back to Canada to get them, La Salle found everything against him. Frontenac, his firm friend, was no longer there, for the king had grown tired of the quarrels between governor and intendant and had recalled them both. The two sent out instead agreed well with one another and also with Laval and the Jesuits.

Governor de la Barre was as weak as Frontenac was strong. He would have liked to make money in the fur trade, but he had no control over the Iroquois who had much control over it. These shrewd warriors were at the very height of their power, having learned their own importance through both French and English trying to keep friends with them. Though they certainly leaned to the British, they were clever enough not to go over for good to either side, but claimed to be a free people who could do as they pleased in their own country.

La Barre was afraid of the Iroquois, and therefore they had no fear of him. He was quite willing that they should go on the warpath against the Illinois, and thereby ruin La Salle, if they would only leave in peace the tribes of the great lakes so that they might bring their beaver skins to Montreal instead of taking them to trade with the English at Albany. Louis XIV. saw before long that the governor of New France was not fit for his post, and brought him home again in three years, sending out an old soldier, Denonville, in his place.

1685. The new governor, like the old, was friendly to the Jesuit party, and there was peace within the colony, but the Iroquois kept up the war without. Denonville did not act honestly either with them or with the Indians friendly to the French. In making terms with the Five Nations, Frontenac had always said that his allies of the Algonquin family must be included in every treaty of peace, but Denonville was weak enough to leave them out. Then he made a raid into the Iroquois country, in spite of pretended friendship, and, worse still, he invited a great number of those whom La Salle had coaxed to settle in the neighbourhood, to a feast at Fort Frontenac, and there held them as prisoners, sending the strongest of the men home to France to row in the galleys.

1689. The vengeance of the Iroquois was terrible; and it fell upon La Salle's old settlement at Lachine. One dark night in August, fifteen hundred painted savages, yelling and shrieking, fell upon the sleeping people, and butchered all the men, women, and children in cold blood, excepting those who were kept alive to be tortured and burned. There were soldiers in camp only three miles away, who marched out to the rescue but were ordered back by Denonville, who had quite lost his head. The country for twenty miles around was laid waste by the Iroquois, and Montreal itself was paralysed with terror. It was then that a great cry went up for the return of Frontenac, and Frontenac came; a man of seventy now, but strong of will as of yore, and the only man who was a match for the Iroquois.

He was too late to help La Salle, who was lying in a nameless grave near a lonely river in Texas. The great explorer had known it was useless to seek aid for his schemes in Canada so long as his enemies were in power there, and leaving Tonty in command of the Fort St. Louis, on the Illinois, he had gone to France for support and had got it. With three vessels and a goodly supply of colonists and stores, he sailed for the Gulf of Mexico, meaning to go up the Mississippi from there, but he passed its mouth and landed at last four hundred miles to the westward, on the shores of the present State of Texas. There he built a fort to protect one part of his people, including the women and children, while he with some of the men tried to reach "the fatal river," as they called it, overland.

1687. Disaster had met La Salle from the first of the expedition. Two of his ships had been wrecked, his followers had died of disease or had rebelled against his authority, but still the strong heart of the man would not give way. It was not the first time he had attempted more than he could do. He grew colder and more silent than ever with the men now trudging the dreary wilderness with him, and two of them at length shot him dead, beside a southern branch of the Trinity River. His murderers were afterwards killed by other members of the party, and but five or six of the whole with the help of the Cenis Indians, reached Fort St. Louis in safety. Tonty had taken a trip from it the year before down to the mouth of the Mississippi to look for his friend and commander, but had found no trace of him.

France and England were at war when Frontenac came back to Canada, so that he had an excuse for waging war against the English colonies whom he blamed for stirring up the Iroquois against the French. He brought back with him the Indians who had been sent over to be galley slaves, and thus made peace with the Iroquois. Though he had too few regular soldiers to make a big war and capture New York, as he would have liked to do, he could command the services of a daring band of *coureurs de bois*, who would bring in troops of Indians, scarcely more wild than themselves, to do his bidding. With these it was possible to make "the little war," by which was meant the springing upon a peaceful settlement by surprise and killing or making prisoners all the people in it, men, women, and children.

1690. One of Frontenac's war parties of two hundred and ten men, half French and half Indians, fell upon the village of Schenectady, in the dead of a winter's night, and within two hours one hundred and fifty souls were killed or taken prisoners. Another band of fifty French and Indians made a raid upon Salmon Falls, a hamlet between

Maine and New Hampshire, where again the sleeping people were made captive if not slain by the tomahawk or Indian hatchet. The third expedition, one hundred strong, made for Casco Bay, the site of Portland, where the English had a fort into which they fled with their wives and families. On the promise of their lives, they surrendered, but the French broke their promise and turned the helpless folk over to the savages.

These raids had the effect Frontenac intended of making the Iroquois afraid to attack the French; but the English colonists were not Iroquois, and the burning of their villages, the massacre of their people, did not lead them to beg for peace. An expedition sailed from Boston that same year under Sir William Phips, and began by plundering Port Royal, the chief place in Acadia, which was not in a state to defend itself; but when thirty-four ships appeared before Quebec on the 16th of October Frontenac was ready for them. His post was strong by nature, and he had made it stronger still by placing towers of stone at the weakest parts of the wooden walls. Phips sent him word to give up Quebec within an hour, but he boldly replied that his guns would answer for him; and answer they did to such purpose that the ships were badly battered while their cannonballs had no effect upon the "city set on a hill." Having failed to make a landing anywhere on their way up the river, the enemy retired in disgust and Canada breathed freely once more.

The English succeeded better in getting the Five Nations to go on the war-path, particularly against the settlements between Montreal and Three Rivers, which were most exposed. There is no braver story in Canadian history than that of Madeleine de Verchères, a girl of fourteen, who with her two little brothers of ten and twelve held the fort on her father's seigneurie against forty or fifty Iroquois, for a whole week, keeping up such a show of spirit that the Indians believed the place to be full of soldiers, and were afraid to attack it.

Frontenac's last expedition was against the Iroquois. He went himself into the country of the Onondagas at the head of twenty-two hundred men, and so great was the fear of his name, the Indians burned their largest town and fled from before him.

One of the most remarkable men of Frontenac's time was Pierre le Moyne d'Iberville, son of the famous Charles le Moyne of Montreal, who had ten other sons, most of whom made their mark in the colony. D'Iberville had been trained in the French navy, and most of his daring deeds were done afloat, but he was one of the party that marched six hundred miles on snowshoes and destroyed three out of the five Hudson's Bay factories, or trading posts, on the shores of that vast sea. His next exploit was to capture the stone fort which Sir William Phips had built at Pemaquid to protect New England; and when that was demolished he sailed off to Newfoundland, where he burned the village of St. John, and many smaller settlements besides, leaving hundreds of poor fishermen homeless in mid-winter. Then he sailed into Hudson's Bay and had a gallant sea-fight with three British ships against his one. D'Iberville beat them all, and destroyed the last fort of the Hudson's Bay Company. He claimed the whole region for France, but it was given back to England by the Treaty of Ryswick in 1697.

Frontenac was seventy-seven when he died the next year in the Château of St. Louis which he had built on the edge of the cliff at Quebec, and where he so proudly received the messenger of the English invader. He had served the land well as a military governor, and had also held his own against bishop and Jesuits. Laval was still in the colony, and he died there about ten years after Frontenac, aged eighty-five;

but he had been succeeded in his office by Bishop St. Vallier, who in 1693 founded the General Hospital of Quebec.

Frontenac lived long enough to see the power of the Iroquois broken, the western tribes firm in their friendship for Canada, the south and west held for France. The dream of keeping the English to the east of the Alleghanies might yet come true.

QUEBEC

PART THIRD

TO THE END OF THE EIGHTEENTH CENTURY

CHAPTER IX

NEW FRANCE SPREADS HER WINGS

URING the thirty years of peace that followed the Treaty of Utrecht, the people about Quebec came to have no ambition beyond raising large families on their long, narrow farms, which, through frequent subdivision among the children, grew still more narrow, for each, of course, must keep a frontage on the river.

Montreal, on the other hand, was the

chief market to which the Indians from the west brought their furs, and with them came also the *coureurs de bois*, who now liked better to be called *voyageurs*. There was a good deal of traffic with Albany, too, in time of peace, so that Montreal was far more in touch with the outside world than Quebec, and not so easily ruled, either by church or state. Her young men went into the woods every year, in spite of the laws against it, and in spite of the complaints of the merchants they left at home that every new post in the western wilds was but a means of lessening the supply of furs brought to Montreal. The governor at Quebec, as military head of the colony, saw the importance of these posts in keeping back English settlers. He was often in league with the *voyageurs*, and shared with them the profits of their trade, so it went on.

1701. Du Lhut had set up a temporary trading post at Detroit in 1686, but it was La Mothe-Cadillac, a gentleman rover, who made a permanent one near the same spot and gathered about him numbers of the Huron and Ottawa Indians from Michilimacinac. His chief end was to keep the English out of the fur trade, and to get into it himself.

The Iroquois were now called British subjects, and they were always trying to make the western Indians sell their furs to the English through them, but it was the aim of the French to prevent this, without falling out with the Iroquois.

Indian wars in the west would spoil the trade for everybody, and for a time it seemed as if the Outagamies, or Foxes, were being stirred up by the Five Nations, with the English at their back, to put an end to the ten-year-old French fort at Detroit. They would have succeded in their purpose had not six hundred friendly Indians come to the rescue. The Foxes were besieged in their turn and defeated with great loss; but their spirit was still unbroken, and two years after the attack upon Detroit they made a raid upon La Salle's old friends, the Illinois. There was a flourishing little French colony among them at Kaskaskia, on the Mississippi, and sixteen miles up the river was Fort Chartres, built by the French from Louisiana. It was made first of wood and earth, afterwards of stone, and it held the northern Mississippi to keep the way open between the two wide-apart wings of New France. But the warlike Outagamies gave the district no peace till the vengeance of the French had pursued them to their homes on the far-off Fox River, and so many of the tribe were killed that they had to join themselves to their neighbours, the Sacs.

M. de Callières had been twenty years in Canada, part of the time governor of Montreal, before he became governor-general, and he brought to his office much experience in colonial affairs as well as the prudence and common sense that were natural to him. An honourable man and a statesman, he did not copy Frontenac, the governor before him, in making "the little war" upon the outlying English settlements, for he declared that these raids did no good, but harm, to Canada. He would rather have attacked Boston and New York with a fleet from France, but the fleet from France never came, while the fleet from England did.

1711. That was during the time of the next governor, Marquis de Vaudreuil, under whose direction the little war was kept up so vigorously that England, Old and New, felt there would be no peace in America till Quebec was taken. The fleet sent for the purpose was commanded by Admiral Sir Hoveden Walker, and a land force was to proceed to Montreal by way of Lake Champlain in order that Canada might be conquered at one swoop. She had only 3,350 fighting men, so that French, as well as English, were sure the expedition would succeed; and well it might, had not the commander-in-chief been utterly unfit for his post. What mattered his array of ships, when not one of his twelve thousand men could pilot them up the St. Lawrence? Unheeding the thick fog in the river, the admiral stupidly persisted in going forward, against the advice of his officers; and his vessels, sailing too close to the north shore, ten of them were wrecked on the reefs of Egg Island. Seven hundred men were drowned, but there were still enough left to have gone on and besieged Quebec, had not Walker's courage failed him. The military commander on board was a coward too, and what was left of the fleet put about and ran home again without doing anything. The land expedition could not act alone, so it too came to nothing; and the Canadians, looking upon their deliverance as a miracle in answer to prayer, held services of thanksgiving.

M. de Callières had followed Frontenac's method with the Iroquois, of whom there were now a number of Christian converts who had been persuaded by their Jesuit teachers to leave their homes in New York and settle in Canada at Caughnawaga, Lake of the Two Mountains, and St. Regis. These, of course, did not care about fighting their own race, nor did their former friends care about fighting them. Besides the missionaries a French officer, called Joncaire, was of great help to the governor in keeping the Iroquois neutral in the wars between French and English. He had been captured and adopted by the Seneca Indians, had married a squaw, and lived among them like one of themselves. Joncaire was often able to quiet their anger when it was rising against his countrymen, and when he could not do that he would send word to the French what the Iroquois were about to do. His half-breed son trod in the same path after his father died.

The Le Moyne family of Montreal had much influence among the Onondaga section of the Five Nations, which, in 1713, became Six Nations by taking in the Tuscaroras from the south. Maricourt and Longueuil, sons of Charles le Moyne, held one after the other the difficult and dangerous post of "consul" to the Onondagas, who christened the former *Taouistaouisse* (little bird which is always in motion), and truly the same title would have applied to any one of the Le Moyne brothers, so full of life and enterprise were they.

Le Moyne d'Iberville succeeded where La Salle had failed. Henri Tonty had begged for help to carry on the explorations of his late commander, but he had not D'Iberville's influence at Court, and therefore it was the latter who sailed from France for the mouth of the Mississippi in 1699. He went up "the fatal river" far enough to decide it was really the one sought; and the best proof was a letter given him by an Indian chief with whom Tonty had left it for La Salle when he came down the stream fourteen years before to look for his unfortunate friend.

D'Iberville built his first fort at Biloxi on the Gulf of Mexico, but the next year he changed his quarters to Mobile. His brother, Bienville, a youth of eighteen, who had come out with him as a midshipman, became Lieutenant of the King and afterwards governor of the colony. He founded New Orleans in 1718.

Louis XIV. took a special interest in the new settlement named for him, but as in Canada, he made the mistake of handing over its trade first to one man then to a company. The emigrants brought out were not of the right sort. They had no desire to turn farmers, but were keen after gold mines and pearl fisheries. To be sure, the soil about Mobile was the reverse of fertile, but there were game and fish in plenty, and the people need not have starved if they had been willing to work. Year after year numbers of them had to be sent to live with the natives, who were noted for never refusing to share their food with the hungry, so long as they had any to share.

Bienville's way of managing the Indians was not always honest, but he had many cares, not the least of them being the letters that his companions in office were constantly writing to France, finding fault with him. It was wonderful what little things the king and his ministers liked to hear when they came from one of their servants about another in Louisiana, Acadia, or Canada.

La Mothe-Cadillac was governor of Louisiana for a time and gave a very poor account of the colony. Certainly, the climate was against it, and before long negro slaves were bought to assist in the growing of tobacco and coffee. Thus was introduced another factor, and one not easy to reduce, into a settlement which was already a curious mixture of soldiers, priests, nuns, beggars, convicts, and *coureurs de bois*. Had King Louis let the Huguenots emigrate there, as they wanted to do, instead of adding their strength to the English colonies, the whole valley of the Mississippi would in time have filled up with a hardy and industrious population, more likely than a few scattered forts to have held it for France.

Since the beginning of the century the walls of Quebec had been strengthened little by little, but they did not yet enclose the whole town, and Vaudreuil was anxious to complete them; but his death in 1725 put a stop to the building for a time. He had served Canada for twenty-one years as governor-general and had been governor of Montreal for seventeen years before that, so he knew the colony well. In his time many ships were built at Quebec for trade with Montreal, Cape Breton, and Prince Edward Island. Card money in place of coins had a run for a couple of years and came in again during the term of the next governor, the Marquis de Beauharnois, who also ruled Canada for twenty-one years. He was a naval officer, fifty years old, when he came out, and the customary squabbling between governor and intendant continued, for indeed the king's minister in France never wanted the two to be friends, because the one was most useful as a spy upon the other. The population of the colony at that time was almost thirty thousand.

Beauharnois did not try to subdue the spirit of enterprise which was abroad in New France, but did what he could to profit by it. He was one of a trading company which built a post at Lake Pepin, on the upper waters of the Mississippi, to collect furs from the Indians of that far-distant region, and he was also a firm supporter of the most noted explorer of his time, Pierre Gautier de la Vérendrye, son of the governor at Three Rivers. He held a small post at Nepigon on Lake Superior, and was thus brought into contact with the Indians from the far west, who told him such wonderful tales of the lakes and rivers in that vast unexplored region, Vérendrye thought he might, by one or other of them, reach the Pacific Ocean.

1732. His three sons and a nephew went with him on his expedition, and there were also a number of *voyageurs*, Indian guides, and the Jesuit missionary, without whom no exploring party was thought to be complete. To take a priest along was a sign that they were not mere *coureurs de bois*, going for their own good, but had at heart the good of the Indians with whom they might trade.

The company followed the tedious canoe route with many portages, that took them by way of the Rainy Lake and Rainy River into the Lake of the Woods, where one of Vérendrye's sons was killed in a fight with those "Iroquois of the West," the Sioux. His nephew died soon afterwards, and most of his men were rebellious and troublesome, as in the case of La Salle, and partly from the same cause—the enterprise was not supported in Canada, and the promised supplies were not sent. More than once Vérendrye had to journey back to Montreal to make arrangements with his creditors. The undertaking was at his own expense, and the only way he could hope to support it was by the fur trade. To control that it was necessary to build fortified storehouses here and there along his route, and to keep these provided with food for the few men left in charge, and with goods to supply the Indians. One such fort was set up on Rainy Lake, another on the Lake of the Woods, two on Lake Winnipeg, and one each on Lake Manitoba and the Assiniboine River. These caught much of the trade that had hitherto gone to the English on Hudson's Bay.

1742. Before this time the spare strength of the Hudson's Bay Company had been spent in sending out ships in search of a north-west passage to the Pacific through the ice-floes of the Arctic Ocean, and the Indians had brought their furs to the Bay of their own accord. Now that the French had made their way into the region and were likely to disturb the traffic, the Hudson's

Bay Company branched out to meet the Indians—first one hundred and fifty miles up the Albany River, then further and further till, before the century closed, their posts were dotted over the whole North-west.

Vérendrye was fifty-seven when his sons left him at Fort Rouge on the Assiniboine, the future site of Winnipeg, to make the remarkable tour upon which they were gone for a whole year. They had but two men with them—Canadians—and they visited among strange tribes of Indians on the banks of the Missouri River in the present State of Dakota.

1743. Going as far as the base of the Big Horn Range in Wyoming, they were the first white men, so far as recorded, to see the Rocky Mountains. After his father's death, in 1749, one of the sons explored the River Saskatchewan.

Like La Salle, these brave *voyageurs* gained nothing for themselves. Beauharnois had favoured their enterprise, but the next governor, La Jonquière, was a miser, and to him was joined Intendant Bigot, who had no objections to spending money, but it must be for his own pleasure or profit. The stealing from king and from people alike that began in their time was kept on until Canada was lost. The forts that the Vérendryes had built, the furs they had collected were all handed over to strangers in the pay of these new rulers, and the pioneers who had led the way into the great North-west died very poor.

NOVA SCOTIA

CHAPTER X

THE FIGHT FOR NOVA SCOTIA

IT was on account of being so easy to reach from the sea that Nova Scotia, the Acadian peninsula, changed masters every few years. The settlements on the St. Lawrence could be invaded from New England only by a long and tedious march through thick, tangled woods; or by an equally long and tedious sail up the great river of Canada, where pilots were needed and where the warlike people along the banks were well able to fight for their homes. Perched on a rock, Quebec could look down with scorn upon the foe; but Port Royal was poorly defended, and the Acadians were not so hardy nor so enterprising as the Canadians, not having had the same amount of Indian fighting nor of fur-trading adventures in the far west.

The men of New England, placed as they were on the Atlantic coast, became bolder by sea than by land, and found their way to Nova Scotia both in peace and in war. In the one case they would trade with the Acadians; in the other they would capture their forts. In the latter event, an expedition would be sent down from Canada to drive out the invaders; or the country would change hands again, when peace was declared. Both France and England used Acadia as a sort of balance, to be thrown in on this side, or on that, when the results of the war in other parts of the world were being weighed and settled.

That was what happened in 1667, when, by the Treaty of Breda, the present Nova Scotia, New Brunswick, and a part of Maine became once more the property of Louis XIV. of France. There were but few settlements besides those along the Bay of Fundy, and Port Royal was the only place that had a stone fort and a garrison; therefore whoever took Port Royal considered that he took the whole country. Sir William Phips did so, in 1690, but he had neither the men nor the means to hold the place after he had taken it, and a French governor came back the next year.

If there were few white men in Acadia, there were plenty of red, mostly Abenakis and Micmacs, among whom the Jesuits had been at work so long they had them completely under control. The Indians were taught that it was their Christian duty to kill the English whenever and wherever they could, and whether or not there was peace between France and England. The priests often led them in person on their raids and persuaded them to save their prisoners for a ransom, instead of torturing and burning them. They made little other attempt to civilise their flocks, thinking it unwise to teach them to read and write, or even to speak French.

If the natives cleared the ground and settled down upon farms, like white men, it would not be so easy to start them off on the war-path against the English. Knowing the Indian character, the Jesuits governed them through their fears and their jealousy. The Abenakis at times grew tired of the war and would have been glad to live at peace with the English. The blankets, hatchets, knives, and so on, they gave in exchange for furs were cheaper and wore better than the French articles, trade being freer in New

England than New France. But the French were determined there should be no peace, and when the Abenakis showed signs of weakening they were spurred on to a new attack which the English would revenge when they could, and so keep the trouble alive. Orders came from King Louis himself that the Indians must be taught that they could make a better living hunting the English than hunting the beaver, for if once the borders were quiet, settlers from the south would push over into Acadia, as the French said they were doing already; for there was a difference of opinion about the boundary line.

The English thought they had a right to the country as far north as the river St. Croix, while the French claimed it as far south as the Kennebec; and in the disputed part lived and reigned the bold Baron de St. Castin, at Pentegoet, on the Penobscot. He had married the daughter of an Indian chief and was a mighty man among his wife's relations, whom he often led to "the little war" against the English, though he was not above making money by trading with the "Bastonnais" in times of peace.

The Marquis de Vaudreuil, governor at Quebec, who had set himself to ruin New England, thought he could kill a sturdy tree by lopping off a few of its outermost twigs. He had one great advantage over the English colonies, in that he could, whenever he chose, call out every able-bodied man in Canada to go to war; and they would have for officers young men of good family, trained in fighting, who thought it beneath their dignity to do anything else. Indeed there was little else for them to do, if they wanted to advance themselves, for trade of every kind was kept among a few, and all the civil offices were given to favourites from France. The English colonists, on the other hand, though far more in number than the Canadians, were divided up into little republics, each jealous of one another and of any interference from the mother country. Virginia, Rhode Island, and Pennsylvania being beyond the reach of French invasion, thought that Massachusetts could look after her own borders ; and the Assembly of that colony was slow in voting money, even for her own defence. Her soldiers were mostly farmers who ran from the plough to a blockhouse when they heard of the Indians coming ; but generally they got no warning.

1704. Besides the smaller raids, when two or three families were taken at a time, and their houses burned, the little war which Vaudreuil kept up, included attacks such as the one upon Deerfield on the Connecticut River, at that time the most northerly settlement of Massachusetts. Three hundred Canadians and Indians went from Montreal by way of Lake Champlain and the Onion River, and surprised the Deerfield people in their beds on a winter night. In one hour thirty-eight were killed, and one hundred and six taken prisoners, to endure the long tramp of two hundred and fifty miles back to Canada. Two dozen of them, women, children, and old people, died from cold and hunger, or were knocked on the head by the way, when they could not keep up with their captors. The survivors were divided among the villages of so-called Christian Indians, to work like slaves till their time came to be exchanged for French prisoners. Some of the children were never given up, but remained savages the rest of their lives, forgetting even the English language.

It was not an Acadian party which had done this particular deed, but it was Acadia that could be struck in return; and Massachusetts, rising in her wrath, sent Colonel Benjamin Church thither with seven hundred men in whale-boats. He began with a raid upon the St. Castin place on the Penobscot, and then sailed to the head of the Bay of Fundy, burned Grand Pré and

Beaubassin and took a number of prisoners to keep for exchange. Three years later another expedition was sent out to take Port Royal, but failed.

1708. When Haverhill, on the Merrimac, was devastated as Deerfield had been, Massachusetts stirred up New York and New Hampshire to help her seek revenge. A fleet sailed from Boston to Port Royal and besieged it for a week, when the French, knowing that their walls were out of repair and that they were as short of food as of powder and shot, gave up their Acadian capital. It was never theirs again, though for long they hoped and planned, by open means and secret, to win it back.

1713. The name Port Royal was changed to Annapolis Royal, in honour of Queen Anne, and by the Treaty of Utrecht, Acadia and Newfoundland were handed over to England, while France was left with a few islands in the Gulf, of which the largest were those now called Prince Edward and Cape Breton. The last was considered the most important, as a gateway to the St. Lawrence, and the French determined to place a strong fortress upon one of its harbours, from which vessels could make raids upon the New England coasts during the next war, and would also have a good chance to retake Acadia. A harbour in Cape Breton would not be ice-bound for half the year, like that of Quebec, and fishing-boats could always take refuge there.

Louisbourg, the stronghold was christened, and more than a million pounds were spent upon its fortifications, which were twenty-five years in building. It was not an attractive site for a settlement, the ground being marshy and the climate damp, but the people of Newfoundland and Acadia who did not want to live under British rule were invited to go there. The poor fishermen of Placentia consented; but the Acadians were too comfortable where they were, and did not care for hewing down trees, when they had made clear fields for themselves by simply building dykes to keep back the high tides of the Bay of Fundy. It would have been better for England either to have insisted upon their going, or to have sent enough troops among them to protect them from their late masters; but England's eyes were elsewhere. It did not suit her to have a strong colony grow up on Cape Breton while Nova Scotia was left empty, and therefore the Acadians were treated kindly to keep them where they were. For years they were excused from taking the oath of allegiance to the British sovereign, and their young folks grew up with the idea that no allegiance was necessary. They called themselves the " Neutral French," but they were not that at all, for they secretly gave help to their countrymen in every way that they could, going so far as to disguise themselves as Indians in order to fight against the English, when war broke out once more.

1744. The commander at Louisbourg sent a force at once to take possession of Canso, but Annapolis held out against him. Governor Shirley, of Massachusetts, had made up his mind that there would be no peace for his colony until Louisbourg was taken, and he resolved to take it, though he had but a few British ships to help him and the troops, which for once the other colonies contributed readily, were quite untrained. Four thousand farmers, fishermen, carpenters, and blacksmiths, with officers who knew no more about war than did they themselves, would not appear to have much chance against that formidable fortress which had been built by the best engineer of the time and had a garrison of thirteen hundred French regulars.

1745. The command of the English was given to William Pepperrell, a good-tempered merchant with a sound business head who knew how to manage men and was popular with his soldiers—a great matter in an army of that sort where every man thought himself as good as his neighbour. The kind of work they had to do when at length they forced a landing upon the island of Cape Breton, severely tried their manliness, but it was not found wanting. Heavy guns had to be dragged on sleds through the marsh, under cover of the night; but once within firing distance of the walls they did good service, and the sallies from the fort to take them were stoutly beaten back. Victory for once fell to the unlearned. The commander at Louisbourg had not been so well chosen as most French commanders were. He foolishly gave up the Grand Battery, facing the entrance to the harbour, and its guns were turned upon the fort. The British ships waiting without captured a French one trying to get in with supplies; and the garrison was short of powder. After a siege of seven weeks New England gained Louisbourg. A fleet that sailed from France the next year was dispersed by storms and could not retake it, while an attempt on Annapolis failed likewise.

1748-1749. The great rejoicing in Boston

when the fall of Louisbourg became known was turned to bitter anger when the fortress was coolly given back to France in the Treaty of Aix-la-Chapelle. It was still there to menace Nova Scotia; and to act as a guard, in some degree, a fortified town was built by the English on Chebucto Harbour. This was called Halifax and made the capital of Nova Scotia. Started after the French manner by a royal decree, colonists were sent out to it, and in a couple of years there were four thousand of them. Around the dwellings was built a wooden wall and a square stone fort was set on the hill.

Though they had now been British subjects for forty years and had enjoyed far more liberty than the French had ever given them, the Acadians kept on being insolent whenever France seemed likely to win back their country, humble when they feared Britain held it for good. Some of them had gone to Prince Edward Island to be under French rule; but they still outnumbered the English in Nova Scotia and looked for support in their disloyalty to the French fort at Beauséjour. The same means that had been used with the Indians were employed to keep the Acadians true to France, notably the Abbé le Loutre, supposed to be a missionary to the Micmacs, but in reality an active agent of the Quebec Government. An ignorant people, devout Roman Catholics, dreaded his threats of putting them out of the Church even more than his threats of letting loose his Indians upon them if they ventured to obey the English.

They had, on the other hand, been well warned what would happen if they continued their double-dealing, but they paid no attention, feeling sure that such easygoing masters would never have the heart to turn them out of their homes. That was what happened at last, however, and a cruel measure it undoubtedly was, but not half so cruel as the Indian ravages from which New England had long suffered, and for which the French were chiefly to blame.

1755. The British began by taking Beauséjour, and soon afterwards all the men living in its neighbourhood were shut up in the fort until such time as they could be carried away with their wives and families. The men about Grand Pré were collected, unarmed, in the church; and in Annapolis and other districts the same plan was followed. About six thousand souls in all were thus captured, taken on board ship and distributed among the different English colonies.

ONTARIO

CHAPTER XI

CANADA HOLDS HER OWN

N board of the French fleet which was scattered in 1746, was the new governor for Canada, Admiral de la Jonquière, so he did not arrive at that time ; nor had he any better luck the next year, when the ship in which he sailed was taken by the English. To fill the gap at Quebec, the Comte de la Galissonière was appointed, a man with a small, misshapen body, but a large, straight mind, of which the colony for two years had the benefit. His first work was to strengthen all the trading posts on the great lakes ; and his second

was to send out Céloron de Bienville in 1749, to take possession of the valley of the Ohio. This he did by burying five plates of lead at the foot of five different trees throughout the district between the head waters of the Alleghany and the banks of the Miami and Maumee Rivers. Each plate bore an inscription to the effect that Céloron in this manner claimed the whole country for the King of France; but what cared the English traders for Céloron and his boundary lines or his plates of lead? They came over the mountains from Pennsylvania and Virginia at the rate of three hundred in a year. Their manners were not so good as those of the French, but their wares were better and cheaper, and on that account most of the natives put up with the ill-usage they got from them and from the land-grabbers who followed in their train.

The French had forts now all the way between Montreal and New Orleans, beginning with the one at Ogdensburg, then called La Présentation, where the Abbé Picquet had a mission to the Iroquois. On Lake Ontario had been built Fort Rouillé (Toronto) and Niagara, to counteract Oswego, by which the English had nearly ruined the trade of Frontenac. Not beyond portaging distance from Presqu'ile, on Lake

Erie's southern shore were the head waters of the Alleghany River. Le Bœuf was built there and Venango some miles farther down the stream. These two were the forts that roused the wrath of the governor of Virginia in 1754, and made him send the afterwards famous George Washington to request their commander to withdraw, which, it is needless to say, he did not do; and at a later skirmish between Washington's men and the French were fired the opening shots of the Seven Years' War.

The Marquis Duquesne, who had come out to replace La Jonquière in 1752, was, like him, an officer in the French navy. His bearing was cold and proud, so that he found little favour with the Canadians, but he honestly did his best, both for them and for the king, his master. Defying the fortified trading posts, the British kept on pushing over into the rich lands of the Ohio, with a broad front that was very unlike the French occupation of a territory. As Duquesne himself put it to an Iroquois: "Are you ignorant of the difference between the King of England and the King of France? Go, see the forts that our king has established, and you will see that you can still hunt under their very walls. They have been placed for your advantage in places which you frequent. The English, on the contrary, are no sooner in possession of a place than the game is driven away. The forest falls before them as they advance, and the soil is laid bare, so that you can scarce find the wherewithal to erect shelter for the night."

1754. Both sides saw that the point for controlling the whole Ohio valley was where the Alleghany and the Monongahela join to form "the beautiful river," and the English had begun to build a wooden fort there when they were driven out by the French, who made a solid one of stone, named after the governor who had planned it, Fort Duquesne.

In times of peace the superior number of the English colonists told, but in war the French commanders had the advantage. They had not to wait for an assembly of the people to vote their supplies or to tell them what they should do, and they were trained soldiers, not men of other trades and professions doing military duty for the time. The English colonies rarely acted together, and always acted slowly, but now the mother country sent troops for their defence, and the small garrison at Fort Duquesne trembled when they heard that General Braddock was coming against them with twenty-two hundred men.

1755. The English army cut a road for itself as it came, through the woods and over the mountains from Virginia, and the line of march, with cannon, baggage waggons, and men on foot was four miles long, though it need not have been more than half a mile. General Braddock was a strict old soldier, brought up to European ideas of fighting, and with but little idea of how it was done in America. He soon learned. His soldiers had almost reached Fort Duquesne, and thought they had nothing to do but batter down its walls with their cannon, when suddenly the front ranks were attacked by enemies they could not see. Every tree had become an Indian, and from a neighbouring ravine a hot fire of musketry began a steady blaze. According to the correct rules of warfare, the British stood firm in the middle of the road, a solid block of red as a target for their foes, and for three hours the fight was kept up, till Braddock, who had had five horses shot under him, ordered a retreat. On the way back he died of the wounds he had received. Much plunder and many prisoners fell to the lot of the French and their Indian allies.

From the papers they found in Braddock's baggage it was learned that the English were about to make an attack upon the French fort at Crown Point on Lake Champlain, and therefore the Baron Dieskau, who had just come out from France with two regiments of regulars, was sent to meet it. The British were commanded by a noted man of the day, called Johnson, who lived in a fortified house on the Mohawk River, among the Five Nations, and had by his honest dealings gained much influence with them. He built a fort at the head of Lake George and another at the nearest point to it on the Hudson River, and it was between these two that he met the Baron Dieskau and beat him badly. For his services he was made Sir William Johnson, and he called the lake fort William Henry, and the river one Fort Edward, after the two grandsons of the King of England, who had so honoured him; but after all he had not taken Crown Point.

That same year Canada got a new ruler, the Marquis de Vaudreuil, son of the previous governor of the same name, and a native Canadian, so he pleased the people. He pleased the Indians too, for he talked to them like a father, and promised to lead them to the little war against the English. That style of fighting was not to the taste of the Marquis de Montcalm, who had been sent out to command the army, an honourable gentleman and a scholar, as well as a brave soldier and most capable general.

1756. Montcalm's first exploit was the destruction of Oswego, on Lake Ontario, the most hated of all the British posts, for it did most harm to the French fur trade. His troops were of the four different kinds employed by the French—"troops of the line" from France ; the marine corps, or colony regulars, in which were many Canadians ; the militia, that included every man in Canada who could carry a gun ; and the Indians. Oswego had not been built to resist cannon, with which Montcalm was well supplied, and by its surrender a large quantity of food, military stores, and sixteen hundred prisoners were gained by the French. Still greater was their gain in the effect upon the Indians, particularly those of the Ohio valley, who had been leaning towards the English. Now all the border settlements of the latter suffered from their raids. Even the Iroquois, excepting the Mohawks, who were kept back by Sir William Johnson, came in crowds to Montreal to show their friendship for *Onontio*, as they called each governor of Canada in turn.

1757. Captain Robert Rogers, a famous New England scout, the tale of whose adventures sounds like fiction, proved himself equal to a Canadian as a partisan officer, or leader of a party acting by itself in "the little war." He got together a band of rangers, used to bush fighting and to enduring every kind of hardship, and for a year or more these were the only "Britishers" who distinguished themselves.

The French were strong in the Lake Champlain district, but instead of attacking them there, and thus striking at their heart, Lord Loudoun, the English commander-in-chief, wasted his time at Halifax, making up his mind whether or not it was possible to take Louisbourg. While his back was turned Montcalm laid siege to Fort William Henry with over seven thousand men. Nearly two thousand of these were Indians, half of them from the mission villages and half from the far west, including even bands of the Sacs and Foxes, whom the recent victories of the French had turned from foes into friends. Besides facing the difficulties that were always springing up between the colony troops and those from France, the general had to keep that ungovernable horde of savages in a good humour by telling them all his plans and pretending to take their advice in everything. A sudden attack suited them better than a siege, and he never knew the minute they might go off home in a huff, like spoiled children, or fall to fighting with other tribes on the same expedition.

Fort William Henry had less than three thousand troops to defend it, even after a small reinforcement came from Fort Edward, whose commander said he could send no more. Volunteer soldiers were not quickly raised in the English colonies. Well skilled in the art of war, Montcalm soon had his cannon placed in the best positions, and for three days they hammered at the fort, whose guns were in bad order and could do but little in return. Small-pox had broken out among the men, women, and children crowded together in so small a space, and on the 9th of August a white flag was hoisted; the firing ceased, and arrangements were made for the surrender.

Montcalm did not care to carry many prisoners into Montreal, where food was scarce, so he agreed to let all the English soldiers go to their own Fort Edward on the Hudson, with the understanding that they were not to fight against the French again for a year and a half, or until an equal number of French prisoners had been received in exchange. With all the honours of war the British marched out of the fortress they had so bravely defended, but the next morning, when they were getting ready to walk to Fort Edward, and some had already started, Montcalm's savage allies lined the road. They began by stealing the prisoners' clothes, and ended by murdering wounded men, women, children—any one who opposed them. The Canadian partisan officers had seen many similar sights on their raids with the Indians, and they calmly turned their backs upon this one; but when Montcalm and de Lévis, the second in command, heard of the massacre they rushed in among the savages and did all they could to put a stop to it; but they were too late.

The troops of the line should have been told off to protect the prisoners, for Montcalm had seen enough of the Indians to know the outrages of which they were capable, and he had also seen enough of the Canadians to know that they would say, " Let them alone ; savages will be savages. If we did not give them their will of the prisoners we could never get them to come to war with us at all."

Montcalm and his officers succeeded in saving four hundred of the unfortunates, bought their clothes and even their lives back from the Indians, and sent them with a strong escort to Fort Edward. Governor Vaudreuil did the same for about two hundred that their captors took to Montreal, and those were sent to Halifax. Vengeance for the massacre was chiefly wrought by the small-pox, which the Indians caught from their victims and carried home to their villages, where it spread with fatal power.

Fort William Henry was burned, but the fighting in that historic region was not yet done. The next year the English sent an expedition under General Abercrombie to make its way through to Montreal, but first it had to reckon with the gallant little Marquis de Montcalm, who held the fort at Carillon (Ticonderoga). It had been begun three years before and was not yet finished, so Montcalm feared that his thirty-six hundred soldiers, though mostly troops of the line, stood no chance against fifteen thousand. He had bands of scouts on the watch in the woods, and one of these came in contact with an advance party of the enemy under Captain Rogers, and was defeated; but the English lost more than they gained in the death of Lord Howe, a better man than Abercrombie. His army, sure of victory, came on with great pomp, sailing down Lake George in a fleet of batteaux to the music of bands and bagpipes, for the Highland regiment, the famous Black Watch, was there over a thousand strong.

1758. Since the fort could not be defended, Montcalm went half a mile from it, and there settled his men, the battalions of La Sarre, Languedoc, Berry, La Reine, Royal Roussillon, Béarn, and Guienne, all in their white coats with facing of different colours—grimy enough before the fight was over. He made them hew down trees in the neighbouring forest that might have sheltered an oncoming foe, and pile their trunks higher than a man's head on the side of the camp that was open to attack. Beyond this were placed the stoutest branches, with smaller ones whittled to sharp points and turned outwards, making a formidable barrier to a bayonet charge, though a few cannon could have easily knocked it over. A few shells would quickly have cleared the enclosure, but Abercrombie had neglected to bring artillery, and that fact gave the victory to France.

Again and again the British charged up the hill against the spiked wall of trees without effect, while the French took deadly aim at them through their loopholes and showed nothing but the tops of their hats. Half of the Black Watch were slain during that hot fight, which lasted for the whole of a long July afternoon. Abercrombie realised his mistake at last and ordered a retreat, leaving nearly two thousand of his men behind him.

There was great joy in Canada when the victory was known, and the soldiers who had taken part made many jubilant verses, such as:—

>"Allons à Carillon
> Allons voir la merveille
> Où chaque bataillon
> D'une ardeur sans pareille
> Fixe, frappe et bat,
> Dans un seul combat
> Où trois mille François
> Chassent vingt mille Anglois."

NOVA SCOTIA

CHAPTER XII

LOUISBOURG TO QUEBEC

THE expedition of General Abercrombie against Montreal was but one of those planned by King George's prime minister, William Pitt, who was putting new life into the affairs of the nation, both at home and abroad. England awoke to the importance of her possessions beyond the seas and was bound to keep hold of them; but Louis XV. cared nothing for the fate of the colony his father had tended with such care. "A few acres of snow in Canada" were of no account in the eyes of a monarch bent upon pleasure only, and the men and money that might have saved a

continent for him were spent in useless wars in Europe. The Court danced and gambled, while the peasants starved. The awakening of France did not come till thirty years later, in her terrible Revolution.

Pitt's plan was to promote men to command who had shown fitness for the sort of work to be done, and not those who had been longest in the service or had powerful friends at Court. So far the French officers in America had shown themselves to be much smarter than the English, and had made the most of the very mixed lot of troops they generally had under them. Now there was to be less difference between the two sides in that respect.

1758. Once more a fleet and an army set out for Louisbourg: the one under Admiral Boscawen, called "wry-necked Dick" by his sailors, from his habit of carrying his head on one side; the other under General Amherst, a good commander though slow. The New Englanders and Nova Scotians had suffered much from French privateers, who made raids upon their ships or their ports and then ran for refuge under the guns of Louisbourg. That fortress was thought by outsiders to be exceedingly strong, but those who had to defend it knew better. Intendant Bigot, the vampire that fed on the life-blood of Canada, had had a hand in the building of its walls, and although the best materials had been paid for, the worst had often been used. The whole was now out of repair and ready to crumble at the first cannonade. Like Quebec, Louisbourg's chief strength lay in her natural situation. It would not be hard to destroy her if once she could be got at, but to get at her was the difficulty. Her best defences were the rocks and breakers of the island coast, for her fighting men were less than four thousand.

The harbour, large and sheltered, could only be entered by a narrow channel defended by batteries on either side and one facing it, across the bay. The British fleet kept guard without, but several French vessels with supplies ran safely into the haven, and now there were twelve warships riding at anchor within, who dared the English to come and get them. One hundred and fifty-seven British vessels there were, including ships of the line, frigates, and transports, carrying more than twelve thousand soldiers. How to land these was the question, in the face of a riotous surf, and an active, ever-watchful foe.

There were four places at which the French feared a landing might be made, and these were specially guarded; but on the 8th of June the British, while sending boats full of soldiers in different directions to scatter the defenders, pulled for the strongest of the four spots, a cove called La Cormorandière. It seemed unprotected to them, but when their boats came within gunshot they received a volley from a solid parapet, so well screened by branches of trees and bushes that it looked like the natural woods.

Seeing the mistake, Brigadier Wolfe waved back his men; but three boatloads of them pretended to think he meant them to go on, and on they went, scrambling ashore at length upon a rocky point that the French thought could not be climbed. There they kept their foothold till only ten of them were left to face seven times their number of French and Indians; but help soon came. Plunging and wading through the breakers with only a cane in his hand, urging on his men to reach the shore, in spite of the deadly surf, and the still more deadly fire of the enemy—that is the first view we get of James Wolfe. He did not look like a nation's hero —a thin, delicate young man of thirty-one, with chin and forehead sloping backwards, tilted nose, and red hair tied in a queue, but with plenty of fire in his blue eyes.

Over a hundred boats and many men were lost before all were landed, but the landing once made, the French retreated to their fortress, fearing that its fall was only a question of time. The British guns and the British trenches drew nearer and nearer to the stronghold as the summer advanced; and one by one the batteries that protected the harbour had to be given up.

Two of the French ships had made their escape, but another, trying to run to Quebec for help, was captured by Admiral Boscawen, lying in wait. The gallant little *Aréthuse* did more harm to the besiegers than any of the others, and she succeeded in running the blockade and getting safely off to France; but the rest were blown up or burned by the fire of the English.

It is easy for men to keep on fighting when they hope for a victory, but the defenders of Louisbourg had no hope. The Chevalier de Drucour held out for seven weeks, knowing that if he kept the English employed at Cape Breton till the season was half over they would not think of going on to besiege Quebec. He would have let them storm his walls sooner than yield, but he thought of the families of the town who had taken refuge in the fort, of how much they had suffered already and how much more they were likely to suffer if the English carried the place by assault; so he surrendered on the 26th of July.

Within two years afterwards not one stone was left upon another to tell where Louisbourg had been. The English did not need it for themselves, when they had Halifax, and there was always the danger of its being given back to France by treaty, as it had been once before. So great was the joy in England and her colonies over the fall of Louisbourg, it more than balanced the disappointment for the disaster at Ticonderoga.

The latter affair was not so soon forgotten by General Abercrombie, and to revive the spirits of his army, he sent three thousand men, under Colonel Bradstreet, to besiege Fort Frontenac on Lake Ontario, where the French were not looking for an attack. The party crossed from the ruins of Oswego, and when once their big guns were brought into position the fort held out but a few hours, for it was not built to resist cannon. By the surrender the English gained guns and armed vessels, provisions, and more than a hundred prisoners, a valuable lot of furs, and a great quantity of goods intended for the posts on the Ohio. The last was most important in view of the expedition against Fort Duquesne.

L

1758. Brigadier Forbes commanded that, a heroic soul in a body racked with pain. He had to be carried in a litter along the rough road which his soldiers and woodmen made in a straight line from Bedford, Pennsylvania, to Fort Duquesne ; but so long as his clever head was able to direct operations he took no heed of his sufferings. He did not use the road Braddock had built, nor copy that general in stringing out his forces to the length of four miles ; but placed the stores and baggage in fortified houses along the route, so that the soldiers could advance quickly, a short distance at a time.

The commander at Fort Duquesne could no longer count on the support of the Indians, who had been won over to make peace with the British ; he could neither feed them nor trade with them, for all his goods had been lost at Fort Frontenac. When his scouts brought him word of the twenty-five hundred men coming against him, he did not wait to receive them, but blew up the walls of his fort, set fire to the ruins, and got safely off with his small garrison.

When the invalid hero arrived with his men on the 25th of November, they built a few wooden huts for their own use, and Forbes christened the place Pittsburg, which has now expanded into one of the chief manufacturing cities of Pennsylvania. The army marched back once more, over the road they had made, carrying with them their suffering leader, who died in Philadelphia the following spring.

The wings of New France were now severely clipped. Canada and Louisiana were still her own, but the country between them was lost and so was her guardian at the door of the St. Lawrence. Montcalm's victory at Carillon and Drucour's stand at Louisbourg had kept the British away from Quebec for a season, but what could now prevent them from sailing there in the spring? Nothing but help from France, and that had been already refused.

Quebec was doing her best in a small way to imitate the Paris fashions. Her upper circle gambled and was gay, while the people cried for bread. Bigot and his friends grew rich, robbing the king with one hand, the habitants with the other. The troops of the line had to be fed on horse-flesh, much to their disgust, but Montcalm made out a humorous bill of fare, containing the different ways in which it could be cooked, and Lévis set his soldiers an example by eating it himself. He was greatly beloved by his men, and much liked both by the governor's party and the general's party between which the colony and the army were divided.

Hitherto the governor of Canada had been also its sole military commander, and Vaudreuil did not like to share the charge with Montcalm, especially when he got orders from France to submit to the general's judgment in military matters. Vaudreuil was an honest man, but weak, and not shrewd enough to see through M. Bigot, who kept friendly with him by flattering his vanity and was left to make money as he chose. The intendant entertained right royally, but the people had to pay for it.

Though small in stature, Montcalm had a handsome face, and there was all the fire of youth in his flashing black eyes, though he was now forty-seven years old. Like many southerners, he had a hot, impulsive temper, and needed a clever, cool-headed friend at his side to keep him out of trouble, but even Lévis often failed to keep the peace between him and Vaudreuil. The governor was inclined to think too highly of himself and his native colony; the general was too apt to care only for the honour of the king's troops and his own advancement in the army.

1759. Montcalm knew that Quebec could not withstand the blows of English cannon, and that if he shut up his soldiers within the walls they would very soon run short of food; so in the spring, when it was known that the English were moving upon Quebec, he laid out his camp from the St. Charles to the Montmorenci. That would prevent the enemy from getting to the weak side of the town, where the land slopes down to the St. Charles River; the high side next the St. Lawrence was thought to need little or no protection. There were more men up in arms against Canada than her whole population, all told; but with little ground for hope, to the last she did not despair, having faith that her religion would save her, or that France would send help.

General Amherst's part in the campaign was played upon Lake Champlain, where he spent the whole season building vessels and repairing forts, as the French blew them up and left them. They still held out at Ile-aux-Noix, a well-fortified island in the Richelieu, and Amherst appeared to be in no hurry to dislodge them in order to advance to the help of General Wolfe before Quebec. It seemed as if the latter were not going to succeed in taking the capital that year, for the summer wore on and nothing was accomplished but the burning of villages and the laying waste of the country on both sides of the St. Lawrence.

The British fleet of seventy ships had come up the river in June, guided by pilots decoyed on board by the hoisting of French colours; but Montcalm thought Wolfe had acted foolishly in dividing his forces. Part of the English army was encamped on the other side of the Montmorenci from the French; part on the island of Orleans, and part at Point Levi. Could the French general have spared the men, he might have attacked any one of these sections before the others could have sent help; but Montcalm had no troops to spare. Eight hundred were off with Lévis in Montreal, watching for the advance of Amherst, and three thousand were with Bougainville, guarding the river above the town against a possible landing of troops from the British ships which had passed upward. Montcalm must play the waiting game—must lie low and see if he could not tempt Wolfe into attacking him. That is what Wolfe had done on the 31st of July, and been badly beaten. His men landed on the Beauport shore, and tried to climb the hill to get at the French camp; but had it not been for a storm of wind and rain that kept the foe from seeing them, the whole British force would have been slain. As it was, they retreated to their boats with heavy loss.

When the month of September came the Canadians began to take heart. True, their capital was in ruins, for the English batteries at Point Levi had shelled it furiously—a useless destruction of property that brought no nearer the possession of the town. If the enemy did not get in soon they would have to give up the siege for the season, or their ships would be caught in the ice and their men left without food in a hostile country.

On the night of the 12th Montcalm took little rest. He felt sure that the English, with such power in their hands and with so daring a leader, would not leave the country without making a last desperate attempt to take Quebec. He walked about his encampment till nearly dawn, and then was roused from a troubled sleep by the booming of big guns along the Beauport shore. Were the English trying again to land there? The question was answered by news that reached him at six o'clock and sent him spurring his horse towards the bridge of boats that was laid across the St. Charles. From there he saw, only too plainly, a body of redcoats drawn up in line upon the plains of Abraham, the high land within a mile of Quebec. Was it a squad or a whole army, and how did they get there ? Probably the gallant general never learned how the British had dropped down the river from their ships above the town ; how they had made the French sentries think their boats were some expected provisions ; how they had climbed the heights by a path so steep that only a small guard had been thought necessary to defend it, and that was soon overpowered.

Fortune favoured Wolfe, and frowned upon Montcalm. The latter should have waited till Vaudreuil sent up the rest of the troops from Beauport; till Bougainville came from Cap Rouge to attack the thirty-five hundred British in the rear ; but he thought it would be a mistake to delay until more of the English got up the cliff and had time to dig trenches. They were already between him and his supplies. So with his forty-five hundred men, white-coated regulars, Canadians, and Indians, Montcalm passed through one of Quebec's gates and out by another, to meet his fate.

He barely gave his men time to take breath till he hurled them against the foe, and of course they advanced in bad order, while the British stood firm, and reserved their fire till the French were near enough to receive it with deadly effect. Within twenty minutes all was over, and the French in full retreat, chased back to the city gates, or over the rough hillside down to the bridge of boats by the redcoats and kilted Highlanders. Without a leader strong enough to rally them, they left their camp in disorder, and never stopped their flight till they had reached the natural fort of Jacques Cartier, thirty miles up the St. Lawrence.

Wolfe and Montcalm both lost their lives in that bloody skirmish; the one dying on the field, the other living long enough to be supported into the town on his horse. Montcalm was buried in a grave made by the bursting of a shell in the chapel of the Ursuline Convent; Wolfe's remains were taken home on a warship, and there is a noble monument to him in Westminster Abbey.

MANITOBA

CHAPTER XIII

THE FIRST FEW YEARS OF BRITISH RULE

HEN news of the battle of September 13th reached the Chevalier de Lévis in Montreal, he lost no time in starting for Jacques Cartier to meet the defeated army. The death of Montcalm had given him the command under Vaudreuil, and his presence put new life into the soldiers. Even the governor began to think he had left Quebec in too great a hurry, and was ready to march back again. New France was not lost in one battle, nor was even its capital, so long as

the victorious British could be kept without the walls.

Bougainville, bitterly regretting that he had not known his dearly loved general was in such dire need of his help on that fatal morning, still held out at Cap Rouge, and was now moving towards the town with his cavalry. Every man carried a sack of biscuits across his saddle for the relief of the starving garrison; but they came too late. Vaudreuil in leaving had told Ramesay, the commandant of Quebec, to make the best terms he could with the enemy; and when there seemed to be no help coming from any quarter, the town surrendered and the British marched in.

Lévis knew that he was playing a losing game; that unless there was a revolution in France, to put the management of her affairs into other hands, Canada was lost to her for ever. Still he resolved to put a stout heart to a steep hill, and for the honour of his country try to save at least a part of her American possessions. His army made many plans for the retaking of Quebec in the spring; but meanwhile it was held by a garrison of seven thousand men under General Murray. Like Wolfe, he had been in the front ranks at the battle of September 13th, but the harder task was left to him of keeping that which Wolfe had taken. The town was in ruins. There was barely a roof left to cover his soldiers ; the winter was coming on ; the country people were unfriendly, and could not be relied upon to bring in provisions, while Murray was short of funds to pay for them. He might have given out paper money, as the French rulers had done for years—paper they never meant to change into coin—but the sturdy, honest young Scotchman preferred to borrow money from his own soldiers. It was surprising how much the thrifty Highlanders were able to lend him.

A part of that kilted regiment was quartered in the Ursuline Convent, one of the few buildings in the town left standing, and they did so many friendly services for the nuns, hauling and cutting wood, drawing water for them, that the good sisters in return knitted them long stockings to draw up over their bare knees. None of the soldiers had clothes warm enough to suit so severe a climate, and there was much sickness among them, which the hospital nuns did their best to relieve.

The habitants held aloof from the town for a time. They would not make friends with the new-comers, feeling sure that in the spring France would send out a fleet and an army to claim her own again. General Lévis, in his winter camp at Jacques Cartier, was kept well posted in Quebec news. He had spies even among Murray's own soldiers, and those of the townsfolk who had been induced to come back and try to rebuild their ruined homes, lost no chance of sending him word about the great amount of sickness in the garrison, the small amount of money and provisions.

Firewood was an urgent necessity for the five months of a Quebec winter, and to procure it the British soldiers had to go to Ste. Foye, two miles and a half from the gates, and draw it in on sleds, to which they harnessed themselves. There were bands of Indians always prowling about, intent on cutting off some of these logging parties, so that each had to have an extra guard of soldiers. Several skirmishes took place during the winter with scouts from Lévis's army, but both sides looked anxiously to the spring for the final settlement of the question, " Who shall own Canada ? "

General Murray's was called military rule, but it was different from what usually passes under that name, though punishment followed crime a good deal more quickly than is possible with a civil government. The " new subjects " were protected in their rights of property, allowed to worship as they pleased, and the Protestant emigrants from the English colonies were kept from lording it over them. Murray struck the keynote for the treatment of the French-Canadians by their new rulers.

The snows that had lain all winter in the narrow, steep streets and among the blackened walls of the town began at length to yield to the April sunshine. The ice-bridge between the town and Point Levi opposite gave way on the 23rd, and the large masses of ice that came floating down the river seemed the forerunners of Lévis and his men. Murray sent all the Canadians out of the town. If he were to be besieged he could not feed them, and, besides, it was not safe to have a strong party within the walls friendly to a strong enemy without.

1760. The French army came in boats from Montreal till they were within thirty-five miles of Quebec, when, finding the outposts well guarded, they marched the rest of the way by land, approaching the town from Lorette and Ste. Foye, the sloping side next the valley of the St. Charles. Murray thought it best to march out of the gates and attack Lévis on the 28th of April, before his men should have time to dig trenches or even to get rested after their long tramp through the half-melted snow. So many of his garrison were in hospital, he had less than four thousand to take out to battle, while Lévis had nearly double the number ; but the English had the advantage in cannon, and also in holding the higher ground, where there were rough hillocks for protection. The fight lasted for two hours. There were more men engaged on each side and more men in proportion killed than at the September battle in the same place, but the result was different. This time it was the British who were beaten and who retreated into the town in disorder. A third of their number were slain at this battle of Ste. Foye, and Lévis now laid siege to the town.

It would have been better for his army if he had kept away from Quebec till sure of the support of French ships, several of which had been caught in the ice and wintered at Gaspé. His victory went for nothing two weeks after the battle, when the weary watchers in the town saw the first sail of the season rounding the island of Orleans. The frigate was afraid to show her colours, not knowing if the British had been able to hold Quebec through the winter, but when she drew close enough to see that the red flag, and not the white, floated from the citadel, she hoisted the same and fired a salute, to which every gun in the town replied.

Lévis's men in the trenches heard the firing and knew that the game was up for them. They retreated as they had come, back to Montreal. Bougainville still held the post at Ile-aux-Noix, but to it was advancing General Haldimand from Lake Champlain, and, knowing that the British were too strong for them, the French left the island fort and made for Montreal.

Murray had done well in Quebec; he did even better on his memorable journey to Montreal with twenty-two hundred men to meet General Amherst, who was coming down from Lake Ontario, but took time to destroy the fort at Ogdensburg on the way. Landing here and there along the river, Murray assured the inhabitants of safety and protection, provided they stayed quietly in their homes, which most of them, having had enough of fighting, were only too glad to do. The forces of the British—seventeen thousand in all—had now gathered about Montreal, from the east, the south, and the west, and Lévis, with his gallant two thousand troops of the line, could do naught but surrender. Late in the autumn the last of the French soldiers were shipped back to France, and a few of the seigneurs and their families who did not want to live under British rule went with them. Bigot and his crew left to enjoy the fortunes they had made in Canada, but they were brought to trial and severely punished.

A later stand was made for France in America by the Indians of the west. The English had never taken pains to be friends with them, as the French had done, and now that the latter were driven out of Canada, the former were no longer afraid of the red men and cared less than ever about their friendship. Sir William Johnson, living among the Iroquois, alone saw the danger, and warned his countrymen to keep on holding councils with the Indians and giving them presents ; but none listened to him.

The French still held Louisiana, as well as Fort Chartres on the Mississippi. From there *voyageurs* engaged in the fur trade roved the western lands ; and they told the Indians that their great father, the King of France, was but asleep ; presently he would awake and drive out the English from all the forts they occupied. It did not take much persuasion to induce the Indians to assist in the driving, and a widespread plot was laid to win back every post in the west.

1763. The leader in the movement was an Ottawa warrior, called Pontiac, who on the 9th of May attacked the fortified village of Detroit and besieged it with eight hundred and twenty men for more than five months. This was a remarkable feat for Indians, who excel in the more rapid warfare of surprise and retreat, but rarely have the patience for a long siege. Within the enclosure of Fort Michilimackinac, as at Detroit, there were a number of small houses, built there at the time when it was not safe to settle without. The homes of a later date were outside, and the Canadian traders and half-breeds who lived in them were on good terms with the scores of Ojibwa and Ottawa Indians camping near by. These warriors invited the British garrison to look on at a game of lacrosse between themselves and a party of Sacs who had just arrived from their hunting-grounds on the Wisconsin River. The English, off their guard, sauntered out of the fort gates, leaving them open, and some squaws sauntered in. During the excitement of the play, the ball was tossed close to an entrance, and the screaming pack of players rushed into the fort, seized their guns and hatchets, which the squaws had hidden beneath their blankets, and massacred every man, woman, and child they could find.

About the same time, according to the plan

of Pontiac, the smaller western posts also fell into the hands of the Indians. Union had given them a fleeting strength, and they used it as savages will—in scalping, burning, torturing, even eating their captives. The forts at Sandusky, St. Joseph, Presqu'ile, Le Bœuf, Venango, Miami on the Maumee, and another on the Wabash, were all taken; but Detroit still held out, though bands of Indians, victors in other places, came to increase the number of the besiegers.

Though he stayed in New York, Sir Jeffrey Amherst was still commander-in-chief of the forces in Canada, but they numbered many less than they had done at the close of the Seven Years' War, most of them having been ordered home. To Colonel Henry Bouquet, a Swiss soldier of fortune fighting for England, is due the chief credit of putting a stop to the war in the Ohio valley. He had been second in command to Forbes in the expedition which changed Fort Duquesne into Fort Pitt, and when the same place was in danger from the Indians Amherst sent him to its relief with some of the Black Watch and a few rangers. After a hard-fought fight he succeeded in beating the red allies at a place called Bushy Run.

Colonel Bradstreet, the same who had destroyed Frontenac, was now sent to the relief of Detroit; but he had not Bouquet's courage and skill in dealing with the Indians, and it was not till Sir William Johnson took the helm that the war was really brought to a close in 1766. If the Iroquois had taken part in it, the results would have been far more serious for Canada; but Sir William had kept so firm a hold upon them that only the Senecas joined the remarkable league. Louisiana had now been ceded to Spain by the French, who, having no longer an interest in the affairs of the continent, let the Indians alone.

Canada numbered seventy thousand souls when she came under British rule, and of these Quebec had seven and Montreal nine thousand. The settlements on the St. Lawrence reached as far down as Rimouski on the south shore and Murray Bay on the north. A change of government could not long depress a light-hearted people, especially when the change gave them more freedom than they had ever enjoyed. There was not a printing-press in the colony until after the conquest, so that books were scarce; but the people did not miss them, for very few were able to read or write. The *Halifax Gazette* had a run for a few months in 1752, but was not published regularly till eight years later, and Quebec had her first newspaper in 1764.

British rule brought free trade in the East, but the Hudson's Bay Company had the sole right to buy furs in the North-west. That fact did not stop adventurers from striking out into the wilderness, chiefly from Michilimackinac, and getting skins from the Indians, to whom they gave far too much liquor in exchange. They did not deal honestly with the natives either, and much disorder followed which hurt the business of the Hudson's Bay Company. But the Company roused itself to extend its bounds to the far north, and sent out Samuel Hearne, who explored the Coppermine River and was the first white man known to have got within the Arctic Circle (1769).

QUEBEC

CHAPTER XIV

THE UNITED EMPIRE LOYALISTS

1766. SIR GUY CARLETON, who succeeded General Murray as governor of Canada, had been a personal friend of Wolfe and his comrade-in-arms during the campaign of 1759. He had also spent the first hard winter with Murray in Quebec, and fought in the battle of April 28th, so that, besides being a tried and capable soldier, he knew something of Canada and the Canadians, and he liked them well. He worked hard for the passing of the Quebec Act in the British Parliament, by which the government of Canada was placed once more in the hands of a governor and council, as it had been under the French, and not into the hands of an assembly of representatives, as the English who were moving in wanted it to be—an assembly in which no Roman Catholic could have a seat, and by which therefore the few Protestants would rule.

Such a Parliament, the first on Canadian soil, had met in Halifax in 1758, but the Nova Scotians were mostly British or New Englanders, educated up to the point of knowing how to govern by their own representatives, as the French Canadians were not. By the Quebec Act, the Ohio country was included in the limits of Canada—an item which opened up the old quarrel with Virginia and Pennsylvania—but Great Britain carelessly signed away the whole region in the next treaty of peace.

It was well for England, if she wished to retain a foothold upon the American continent, that she let her " new subjects " in Canada keep their language, their religion, and most of their laws just as they had been before the conquest. Her " old subjects " in the southern colonies, so soon as they no longer needed her strong arm to beat off the French from their northern, the Indians from their western borders, forgot past favours and remembered only present grievances. When they broke into open revolt, they counted upon the French Canadians siding with them, but few of the new subjects did. The Jesuits, to be sure, favoured the movement, but their order had lost its power since the Pope had suppressed it in 1773, and the rest of the clergy, as well as the seigneurs, stood firm for British rule. They well knew that the Americans, if successful in gaining their independence, would never put up with an established Roman Catholic Church, nor continue the old feudal system of holding land.

1775. Most of the habitants, as the country people were called, refused to fight either for England or against her, but those in the Lake Champlain district sided openly with the troops of Congress when Ticonderoga and Crown Point fell into their hands. These forts the Americans took by surprise, before their garrisons knew there was any war ; but not so the one at Chambly, whose commander yielded disgracefully, without a struggle. St. John's, though weaker by far, stood a siege of seven weeks before it, too, surrendered ; and thus the way was left open for General Montgomery and his troops of Congress to march upon Montreal.

That city had then about thirteen thousand people, many of whom had come from New York or New England since the conquest, and these of course looked upon the invaders as their friends. Here was a chance to do away with the Quebec Act, they thought. The original French citizens had no choice in the matter, for they knew that their town could not be defended, so they made the best terms they could with Montgomery. Three Rivers too sent word that she would submit to his rule, and the Americans were sure that Quebec would do the same. She might have done so had it not been for her gallant governor. Sir Guy Carleton stayed on in Montreal till just two days before Montgomery arrived, on November 13th, and when he gave up hope of holding that town he made all haste down to Quebec, going in disguise as a habitant on board of a coasting vessel. He arrived none too soon.

Colonel Benedict Arnold, whom Congress had sent to unite with Montgomery, was already before Quebec, having brought six hundred and fifty men from Casco, now Portland, Maine, a six weeks' march by the route of the Kennebec and Chaudière Rivers.

Quebec had a garrison of eighteen hundred, made up of British soldiers and sailors, and French Canadian volunteers. When Montgomery joined Arnold, the besiegers had about the same number of men, but they reckoned wrongly when they counted upon getting help from within the walls. The first thing Carleton did was to turn out of the gates all the citizens who were in favour of giving in to the Congress troops. Those who remained were to be relied upon. England was a long way off; she had let them alone and had not been unkind to them. The "Bastonnais" were near, and enemies of old standing; they should not take Quebec.

Montgomery knew that help would come to Canada from Great Britain in the spring, so soon as the ice was out of the river; therefore Quebec must be taken in the winter, which was now well advanced. He had not cannon enough to knock down the walls; the only chance lay in a surprise. The defenders also knew that a sudden attack in an unexpected quarter was the one way by which the enemy could get in; and though their numbers were too few to guard every possible approach, they kept constantly on the watch, sleeping in their clothes, ready to rush from one point to another at the first alarm.

On the last night of the year, the Quebeckers knew there was something on foot, because they saw rockets going up from below the cliff to the west of the town. Montgomery was thus letting Arnold know that he had started to carry out the plan which they had formed. This was to make a pretence of attacking the walls from the Plains of Abraham, to draw the garrison off in that direction, while the real attempt was being made in the Lower Town. Arnold was to advance upon it from St. Roch, the suburb round the corner of the cliff, near the St. Charles River, while Montgomery marched down the bank of the St. Lawrence into Champlain Street. The forces were to meet, storm Mountain Hill together, and force their way into the Upper Town; but the meeting did not take place.

1776. Carleton had ordered three barricades with cannon upon them to be set up in the Lower Town—one at either end of the street called Sault-au-Matelot, and one at the western end of Champlain Street. It was about four o'clock on the morning of New Year's Day that Montgomery and his men drew near the last-named barrier. It was pitch dark and a mixture of snow and rain was falling. Everything was so quiet they thought they were going to surprise the post, but when they came near enough there was a blaze of cannon and musketry; Montgomery fell dead along with a dozen of his men, and the rest retreated in disorder.

Arnold, advancing to the other side of the town, had no better luck. With his seven hundred men he got as far as Sault-au-Matelot Street, but the guard was on the watch there also; he was wounded in the first attack and had to be carried to the rear. His second in command succeeded in forcing the first barricade, but was caught in a stinging fire from the houses between it and the second, so that he had to surrender, and more than four hundred of his men were made prisoners.

The Americans did not again try to take Quebec by surprise, but Congress sent more troops and the siege was still kept on, in spite of the ravages of small-pox among the men. There was much sickness in the town too, but help came for it at length on the 6th of May, in the shape of a British frigate, soon followed by another and a sloop of war with reinforcements that made the Canadians able to march out of their gates upon the foe. But the Americans did not wait to be attacked; they retreated so quickly that even some dinners were left, uneaten, behind them.

A fight took place in May at the Cedar Rapids of the St. Lawrence, where three hundred and ninety Americans surrendered to about the same number of English and

Indians. An American force tried to take Three Rivers in June, but was defeated by a like number of French Canadians and British regulars. The Congress troops had held Montreal all the winter without opposition, but in the early summer they thought it safer to draw back to Lake Champlain.

Sir Guy Carleton forthwith set to work to build a fleet upon that lake, to replace the one destroyed by the Americans the year before, and, if possible, to regain the forts upon it. The summer was over before his ships were ready, but on the 11th of October, along with a number of Indians in canoes, he gave battle to Arnold and defeated him. The Americans destroyed Crown Point, but Ticonderoga was afterwards retaken by the British, so that Canada once more held the lake and was freed from her invaders.

1778. Governor Carleton was succeeded by General Haldimand, who planned and partly made the citadel at Quebec. It was he, too, that began the system of canals on which Canada prides herself to-day. Those that overcame the Cascade, Cedar, and Coteau Rapids of the St. Lawrence were the first canals in America.

Being at war with Spain, France, and Holland, as well as with her revolted colonies,

Great Britain had her hands too full with her foes to remember her friends. The faithful among her old subjects in America were not encouraged in their loyalty, but left to be bullied and beaten, tarred and feathered, robbed and even killed by the party who wished to break all connection with England. Canada opened wide her doors to receive these refugees from the States, who were called United Empire Loyalists. Among them was the greater part of the Mohawk nation, who were given lands upon the Bay of Quinté, and on the Grand River, flowing into Lake Erie, where their descendants abide till this day, though it is doubtful if there is a full-blooded Iroquois among them.

1783. The year that the treaty of peace between England and the United States was signed at Versailles, a number of Montreal merchants formed the North-west Company and entered into the fur trade in the region where the Hudson's Bay Company had been supreme for over a hundred years.

1786-1792. Captain Cook, famous for his voyages round the world, was sent by England, in 1778, to the Pacific coast of what is now British Columbia to see if there was a channel likely to lead through to the Atlantic, but he did not find even the Straits of Juan de Fuca, though he was as near to them as Nootka Sound, Vancouver Island. He got so many costly furs from the Indians there that other voyagers were encouraged to go out, and one of these, Captain Meares, built the first vessel launched upon the Pacific. It was called the *North-west*, and could carry forty tons. He also set up a fortified storehouse at Nootka, but it was taken by the Spaniards, who claimed the whole coast on account of voyages that had been made to it by their sailors. Captain George Vancouver was then sent out to make the Spaniards leave Nootka, which they did, and the English claim to the whole coast of British Columbia was made good.

Meanwhile the U. E. Loyalists had kept on pouring into Canada. Those whose courage, or whose cash, could only carry them a little way over the border, settled near Montreal, in the Eastern Townships; but many went on up the St. Lawrence in open boats, camping out on shore by night, and took up land to the north of Lake Ontario. They founded Kingston in 1783. Others crossed the Niagara River from New York State, laying out their farms along the southern shore of the lake; and this was the beginning of Upper Canada.

1783. About twenty thousand U. E.

Loyalists came from the New England States into the Acadian country, where they settled in the valley of the river St. John and founded the town of that name. The next year the separate province of New Brunswick was made, and two years after that its capital was chosen in Fredericton, which had been founded by the U. E. Loyalists in 1784. The fur trade, that had so long been Canada's chief support, now began to give place to lumber. The tall forest trees of New Brunswick made the best possible masts for the ships of the king's navy.

Nova Scotia also got her share of the new colonists, and they increased her desire for the things of the mind. Even in 1788, "the hungry year," King's College was founded at Windsor, and four years later it became a university, the first in Canada. In Prince Edward Island, named from the Duke of Kent, father of Queen Victoria and commander of the British forces in America, and also in Cape Breton, the U. E. Loyalists mixed well with the Scotch Highlanders, who had begun to emigrate in large numbers to both islands in 1773.

Many of the Loyalists had been very well off in their old homes, but they cheerfully endured the hardships that cannot be avoided in the opening up of new settlements. The British Government gave them help after a time, supporting some of them for three years, until their farms could keep them, and giving them cows and implements for clearing and tilling their lands.

1791-1793. When the Revolution came to France, the French Canadians were heartily glad they had nothing to do with it. A people devoted to church and king, they could look only with horror upon the overthrow of both. The Quebec Act satisfied their ideas of government, but naturally the new settlers to the westward, who had been used to send members to an assembly, did not like it, and the result was that a division was made between Upper and Lower Canada. Sir Guy Carleton, now Lord Dorchester, came back as governor-general over all the provinces, each having a lieutenant-governor of its own. The first for Upper Canada was Colonel J. G. Simcoe, who left his mark in the roads he laid out as a result of walking and paddling throughout his province. Dundas Street from Toronto to London, with its continuation, the Governor's Road and Yonge Street from Lake Ontario to Lake Simcoe were opened up with a view to giving access to the new capital of Upper Canada which he had founded—Toronto, then called York. The first assembly for the province had met at Niagara, but that was thought to be too near to the United States. It was during Simcoe's time that slavery was abolished in Upper Canada. There had never been many negroes in the province, but their numbers were largely increased, as the years went on, by runaway slaves from the United States, who were protected in a genuine "land of the free."

1796. Lord Dorchester and Simcoe were recalled in the same year.

ONTARIO

PART FOURTH

TO THE END OF THE NINETEENTH CENTURY

CHAPTER XV

THE WAR OF 1812-14

1807. In the early years of the nineteenth century Great Britain was much troubled by her sailors deserting to the American navy, where the rules were not so strict and they received more pay. Her right to search United States ships for deserters was bitterly denied by their captains, who often coaxed English sailors to work for them. When the British ship *Leonard* caught up to the U.S. frigate *Chesapeake*, and told her to give up the English sailors among her crew, she refused to obey, and therefore got a broadside from the *Leonard's* guns, whose sailors then boarded her and took off the deserters by force. This was done in time of peace and the Government in England blamed the doers of it, but the ill-feeling between the two nations kept on getting stronger, and five years afterwards it burst into open war.

Canada had hitherto felt only the benefits of being a British colony; now she was called upon to bear some of the ills. She had no quarrel with the United States, but was attacked by them as the weakest and nearest part of a great empire; and most nobly did she rise to the defence. The result of the good treatment given to the Indians in Canada was shown by the way they came forward to fight her battles, particularly the Mohawks, whose name had once spread terror throughout her borders. The Shawnese came to the front too, a band which had been driven from their homes on the Wabash River by the Americans and burned to avenge their wrongs. The chief of this tribe was called Tecumseh—a fine-looking man of thirty-five, brave, as many Indians were, but wise and kind-hearted, as many were not, he kept his warriors from scalping and from other savage tricks. Sir James Craig had been appointed governor-general of Canada when it seemed likely that there would be a war with the United States, because he was a good soldier, but he made himself very unpopular with the people, ruling them as he would a regiment. Prompt and decided in everything he did, Governor Craig would have been a capital man for the head of affairs when the war really did begin, but by that time he had been replaced by Sir George Prevost, a general too, but not a good one, and most of the Canadian disasters were due to his slowness and bad management. Happily, some of those who had control under him were wiser and more daring. There was General Brock, for example, whose name will be held in high honour by Canadians when Prevost's is long forgotten.

Brock was a tall, robust man of fifty-two, who had been ten years in the country and knew how to get on with the Canadians better than most Old Country officers. He did not expect the militia to be like regular soldiers, and when they could be spared he let them go home to attend to the work on their farms. He was lieutenant-governor of Upper Canada, where most of the fighting took place, but the whole country leaned on him; his spirit put confidence into the soldiers wherever he appeared, and he only lost one man by desertion during the three years of his command.

It was the Niagara peninsula which the United States longed for—that fertile triangle of country which follows Lakes Erie and Ontario to the southward—but they did not doubt that the whole of Canada would speedily become theirs; for was not England fighting for her very life against the all-conquering Napoleon, and what could Canada do with her four hundred thousand people opposed to the six millions in the United States, and with but five thousand regular troops to defend a frontier of seventeen hundred miles? She soon showed what she could do.

1812. On the 17th of July, at the very opening of the war, the post at Michilimackinac was taken by surprise by a band of fur-traders, and Canada thus got control of Lake Michigan. No more than in 1776 did the Canadians jump for joy at the idea of becoming citizens of the United States. General Hull, who had crossed the river from Detroit on the 12th of July, camped near the village of Sandwich, but he found his proclamation about the liberty he had brought to a down-trodden people treated with scorn, and when it came to fighting he was badly beaten by Tecumseh and his band. General Brock followed the Americans back to Detroit and took possession of that town on the 16th of August. Its surrender was followed by that of twenty-five hundred troops and the whole State of Michigan.

Their former experience made the Americans hesitate about attacking Quebec; Nova Scotia and New Brunswick were safe, because New England did not approve of the war and took no part in it; it was the nine hundred miles between Quebec and Detroit that were threatened. The United States troops tried to place themselves firmly on the St. Lawrence, so that they might keep supplies from reaching Upper Canada. It seemed easier to starve her out than to fight her, though Brock had under him only thirteen hundred men, of whom the half were Indians.

He had less than a thousand with him in October at Fort George, which faced Fort Niagara at the mouth of the river, when he heard that fourteen hundred Americans had crossed in the darkness and had made their way to a strong position on Queenston Heights, below the falls. Brock rode to the scene in hot haste, but while leading his men up the steep hill to dislodge the invaders, he was shot through the breast and died almost at once. His last words were, "Push on the York Volunteers!" and the York volunteers did push on, driven mad by the death of their beloved general; but it was not until more men came up from Fort George, to raise their numbers from six hundred to a thousand, that the Canadians, under General Sheaffe, stormed the heights and drove the Americans backwards over the steep bluff up which they had climbed. Nine hundred and sixty of them preferred to surrender as prisoners. This victory did much towards giving the Canadians confidence in their power to defend their borders, even against a superior force; and the tall stone monument erected to General Brock, on Queenston Heights, keeps the memory of it ever green.

The third as well as the second landing of American troops on Canadian soil took place on the Niagara River, this time above the Falls, where again they crossed by night, hoping to take Fort Erie at the head of the stream; but Fort Erie refused to be taken.

Canada needed all her land victories to make up for the losses England was having at sea. Her best ships were busy near Europe, and those that came to the American war were mostly old and out of repair. Their guns could not carry so far as those of the United States, whose gunners quickly found that they could batter a British ship to bits while keeping out of range of her cannon ; or if she sailed too fast for them, they had plenty of home ports to run into for refuge. In the first five sea-fights of the war the Americans were victorious, but in each case the United States vessel was the heavier of the two, carried more guns, and had a larger crew.

1813. The first battle of the new year took place in the west, where the whole country had been in the hands of the Canadians since the fall of Detroit. A body of Kentucky riflemen trying to retake it were met and defeated on January 23rd at Frenchtown, on the Raisin River, by a somewhat larger force of British. Seldom had Canada the advantage in numbers. Her troops on the Niagara frontier were but half so many as those across the river ; and there were twenty thousand men in arms ready to be poured into the country between Kingston and Montreal, where there were less than five thousand to oppose them.

But battles are not always to the strong. When the Americans had crossed the St. Lawrence on the ice and made a raid upon

Brockville, robbing houses and taking off peaceful villagers as prisoners, they were repaid by an attack on the fortified town of Ogdensburg, further down the river. Major Macdonell of the Glengarry Highlanders was the hero of that exploit, leading four hundred and eighty men of different regiments. They surprised the garrison, took seventy-five prisoners, burned the barracks and four war vessels, but did no harm to citizens or to private property.

From Sackett's Harbour, opposite Kingston on Lake Ontario, came most of the American war vessels that did damage to the Canadians, and it would have been taken at the first but for Prevost's want of enterprise. Twenty-five hundred men sailed from there to York (Toronto), a defenceless village of less than a thousand people, but then, as now, the capital of Upper Canada. They burned the public buildings, and took away much plunder from private houses; then crossed the lake to the mouth of the Niagara River; but the Canadians blew up Fort George, and deserted all the other frontier posts at their approach. The garrisons of these, joined together, made up an army of sixteen hundred men, under General Vincent, who ordered their retreat to Burlington Heights at the head of Lake Ontario. The Americans followed them as far as Stoney Creek, a tiny stream running into the lake about seven miles from the Heights, and there they encamped.

On the night of June 5th, under cover of the darkness, seven hundred of Vincent's men, led by Colonel Harvey, fell upon the American force, five times larger than their own, and completely routed it, took the two leaders prisoners and more than a hundred men besides. The invaders retreated towards the Niagara, and gave up all the posts they had taken upon it except Fort George. The Canadians advanced as they retired, and two hundred Mohawks from the Grand River and Caughnawagas from the St. Lawrence came along to help them.

Five hundred Americans sallied out of Fort George one dark night in June, bent on surprising the Canadian outpost at Beaver Dam; and they would surely have succeeded in their plan but for the brave act of Laura Secord, a farmer's wife of the neighbourhood, who walked nineteen miles through the woods and swamps, past the pickets of the enemy, and warned the British of the proposed attack. So it came to pass that it was the Americans who were surprised by falling into an Indian ambush, and when Lieutenant Fitzgibbon appeared and demanded their instant surrender if they would be saved from massacre by the savages, they thought they were surrounded by a large force and gave themselves up as prisoners. This was rather awkward for Fitzgibbon, who had only fifty men, but he did not let the enemy know that, and he managed to prolong the business of the surrender until another party of British soldiers came to keep him in countenance.

The Canadians now returned to the Niagara frontier to be the attackers, not the attacked. They captured Forts Schlosser and Black Rock on the American side early in July, but the same month saw a number of their vessels taken by the fleet from Sackett's Harbour, and saw also another burning and robbing raid upon York. British boats were victorious on Lake Champlain; but the hottest fight of the year was upon Lake Erie on September 10th, when Captain Barclay, with six ships, met Commodore Perry with ten smaller ones, and the Canadians were defeated. This gave the Americans control of Lake Erie, and the power to shut out supplies from Detroit, so General Proctor decided to give up that post, which the Canadians had held for a year, and make his way back into Canada with his four hundred British and eight hundred

Indians under Tecumseh. He was followed by an army of three thousand Americans, and a battle was fought on the 5th of October at Moravian Town, an Indian settlement on the Thames. The British had no faith in their leader, and they ran away after the first attack; but not so the Indians, who stood steadfast with their brave chieftain. Tecumseh was at length shot dead, and then his tribesmen scattered, while the victors burned Moravian Town, and they held Amherstburg until the close of the war.

This defeat in the west was balanced by victories in the east over the two American armies that were marching upon Montreal. Three hundred French Canadian volunteers were foremost in the famous fight at Chateauguay, where ten times their number were defeated. By a clever blowing of bugles and yelling of Indians the United States troops were led to think themselves in the middle of an immense army, and they fled in great disorder. The other victory was at Chrystler's Farm, above the Long Sault Rapids of the St. Lawrence, where the invading army of three thousand was met and beaten by eight hundred British on November 12th.

The month of December left scars on the banks of the Niagara. The harmless village

of Newark was burned for no cause by the
New York militia, and its old people,
children, and invalids turned out homeless
on a cold winter night. That cruel deed
made the Canadians very angry, and they in
their turn crossed to the American side and
burned every place from Lewiston to Buffalo.

The British defeats at sea of 1812 were
not continued in 1813. It was in the month
of June, in the latter year, that the well-
matched battle took place between the
Chesapeake and the *Shannon*, which crowds
from Boston went out in pleasure boats to
see. They had the displeasure of seeing
their frigate taken in about ten minutes and
towed off as a prize to Halifax.

1814. Four thousand United States troops
on the way to take Montreal in the spring were
stopped by three hundred and forty Canadians posted in a strong two-storey mill on
the Lacolle River, a branch of the Richelieu.
Oswego was taken by the Canadians in May,
but Fort Erie was lost to them in June.
They were beaten also at Street's Creek near
Chippewa, but made up for that by covering
themselves with glory at Lundy's Lane.
That battle was fought near Niagara Falls;
it lasted from nine o'clock at night till mid-
night on July 25th, and was the hardest
fought fight of the whole war. The

Americans were double in number to the Canadians, and both sides claimed the victory, but the Canadians held their ground, while the Americans retreated to Fort Erie. The British failed in an attempt to dislodge them from there, but on November 5th the Americans retired to their own side of the river, for the war was over. Its last scene in Lower Canada was the failure of Sir George Prevost to take Plattsburgh on Lake Champlain, for which he was greatly blamed.

The United States did not get off scot-free for the damage she had done to Canada. When Great Britain had beaten Napoleon, and was free to turn to America, she sent a fleet to blockade and bombard the Atlantic ports of the United States. The Capitol and other public buildings in Washington were burned in return for what had been done at York. At the very close of the war the British army lost two thousand men before New Orleans; but the Treaty of Ghent brought peace and goodwill on Christmas Day. Neither side kept anything that had been taken, so that the war left boundary lines where they had been before; but the United States had suffered terribly in her commerce and shipping, while Canada had gained in patriotism and in self-reliance.

NEW BRUNSWICK

CHAPTER XVI

MISGUIDED PATRIOTS

AFTER the war was over Canada went forward at a quick march. The St. Lawrence was just two years behind the Hudson in having steamboats. The *Accommodation*, which made the first trip between Quebec and Montreal in 1809, was designed by John Molson, and her hull was built on the river bank behind his brewery in Montreal. The first steamship to cross the Atlantic was built in Quebec in 1831, and called the *Royal William*; the famous Cunard line was started in Halifax, but the first Atlantic liners owned in Canada belonged to the Allans of Montreal.

The Rapids of St. Louis, which had barred

the way to the west for Jacques Cartier and every later voyager, were overcome by the Lachine Canal in 1821, and even Niagara Falls were surmounted by the building of the Welland Canal, eight years later. Vessels now sailed without hindrance from Quebec to the head of Lake Huron.

1825. New Brunswick had a set-back in the terrible forest fire that began at the Bay of Chaleur and spread over the country until eight thousand square miles of woods were burned. Two thousand people were left homeless, and over a hundred were either burned or drowned in the waters on which they had set out for safety in rafts too insecure. Even the fishes in the streams, the seagulls, the snakes in the woods, died from the intense heat, and many cattle were lost that had no stream near to run into and save themselves. Help for the sufferers came in from the United States as well as from Great Britain and Canada, to the amount of £43,607. Fredericton, New Brunswick, was half burnt up the same day, though not in the same fire ; and three times has St. John's, Newfoundland, been laid in ashes, the last time in 1892. Vancouver, British Columbia, had her fiery trial in 1886, when fifty lives were lost and only four houses left standing; but the help that one province gives to

o

another on these occasions binds them all more closely together.

New Brunswick College, Fredericton, dates back to the first year of the century, and the free schools of Lower Canada to the second, while McGill College, Montreal, was founded in 1813. Public schools were started in Upper Canada in 1816, and in 1827 Toronto stepped forward with her university. Nova Scotia, whose chief support had been hitherto her fisheries, found a new outlet for her energies in coal-mining, begun at Stellarton, though coal had been shipped from Cape Breton a hundred years before. The first railway in Canada was a line of fourteen miles between the St. Lawrence and the Richelieu. It was begun in the first of the two Cholera Years, 1832 and 1834. That dire disease was brought to Quebec on an emigrant ship from Ireland, and it carried off its thousands in the two summers.

The rush of emigrants continued, but no increase, either in population or in prosperity, made any difference to the Colonial Office in London, usually spoken of as " Downing Street," from the place where it is. The rulers there were anxious to do right by the colonies, but they did not understand that they had passed the kindergarten stage and were ready to enter the school proper.

True, they elected members to their assemblies, who were supposed to manage the affairs of the country, but these were really in the hands of the Council in each province. The members of that body held office for life, and when once they got in they did not care whether what they did pleased the people or not. Each new governor that came out depended on the Council for advice, and through him it managed to keep control of all public offices and lands, as well as of the money collected in custom duties. The councillors were not robbers, like Bigot and his crew, but they loved power, and were bound to have it all locked up in a certain little circle composed of themselves and their friends. In Upper Canada this clique was called " The Family Compact."

The governors of the period, too, were honest men ; not one of them tried to get rich at the country's expense, and several of them were personally popular with the Canadians—the Duke of Richmond, for example, the worst ruler of the lot, whose death from the bite of a tame fox caused great grief in the colony. He and all the rest came out with the idea firmly fixed in their minds that their first duty was to see that the Canadians obeyed orders from Downing Street, even about their smallest local affairs, though the postage on a letter to England was four or five shillings, and it took weeks to get there.

The same kind of mistakes had ended in the revolt of the thirteen colonies, but British America was too well mixed with U. E. Loyalists to think of following their example. What each province wanted was to have its Council composed of men not only elected by the people but responsible to the people for what they did ; holding their places only so long as they kept the public confidence and were re-elected. That is what is meant by Responsible Government, and that is what Canadians enjoy to-day ; but in the year of Queen Victoria's coronation it was not so much a matter-of-course as it was in the year of her Diamond Jubilee.

One standing grievance of the Reformers was the way in which lands set apart for the clergy were given to those of the Church of England alone, though there were in the Canadas more Presbyterians and Methodists than Episcopalians, and more Roman Catholics than all other denominations joined together. This was a point upon which William Lyon Mackenzie had much to say. He was a Scotchman, and the editor of the *Colonial Advocate*, published in Toronto. Some of his remarks about the land laws, the Post Office, the way in which education was discouraged, and public meetings for the discussion of politics forbidden by the Family Compact, were highly displeasing to the friends of that body. One light June evening in 1826, when Mackenzie was out of town, fifteen young men, who considered themselves gentlemen, broke into his printing office, smashed his machines, and threw the types into the bay. These "kid-gloved roughs" were fined, and Mackenzie, who had been on the point of giving up his paper because it did not pay, was able to keep it going on the strength of the £625 damages he obtained. The ill-usage he had received made him a hero in the eyes of his townsfolk; he was elected to the Assembly, and when "muddy little York" had twelve thousand inhabitants and called itself the City of Toronto, William Lyon Mackenzie was its first mayor (1834).

The Family Compact had so much power they could generally have members that pleased them elected to the Assembly, and these felt bound to do their bidding. Mr. Mackenzie did not please them, and therefore they had him expelled three times, and three times the people sent him back again. The excuse the Tories made for their tyranny was that so many Americans, drawn by the cheapness of land, had come into Upper Canada, there was danger of its being annexed to the United States; and that their party, being mostly U. E. Loyalists, were the best guardians. In their determination to give England her due, they forgot what was due to the colonies. A commissioner was sent out from Downing Street to look into the complaints, but the only result of his report was that the Reformers were told that they could not have Responsible Government; that if the Assembly refused to vote money to be spent by the Council, the latter could take it out of the public funds without asking leave.

Some of the Reformers, sure that they had right on their side, believed that sooner or later Downing Street would become sure of it too, but Mackenzie could not wait. Fifteen hundred men put down their names on his list as being willing to take up arms for their rights—provided they could get the arms. There were four thousand muskets stored in Toronto City Hall; these must be taken by surprise. Sir Francis Bond Head, the lieutenant-governor of Upper Canada, had sent away all the regular troops to Lower Canada to quell the uprising there, refusing to believe that there was any trouble at his own door, though he was well warned by Colonel Fitzgibbon, the hero of Beaver Dam.

1837. Seven or eight hundred men met Mackenzie at Montgomery's Tavern, on Yonge Street, a few miles out of Toronto, but they were badly armed, and before they could march into town the bells rang out an alarm. Fitzgibbon mustered the volunteers to defend the City Hall and remove the arms it contained to a safer place. Help came from Hamilton too, under Colonel, afterwards Sir Allan, Macnab, who marched out Yonge Street with five hundred militiamen and quickly routed the rebels on Montgomery's Farm.

Mackenzie made his escape to Buffalo, New York State, whence, buoyed up by the sympathy given him, he and his friends established themselves on Navy Island and pretended to rule Canada from there. The little side-wheel steamer *Caroline* went back and forth between the island and the American shore carrying provisions to the rebels, but one dark winter night a party of Macnab's "Men of Gore," who were guarding the Canadian side, rowed across the swift and dangerous current, seized the *Caroline* as she lay at her wharf, put the crew ashore, set the steamer afire, and sent her all ablaze over the Niagara Falls. The rebels were thus starved out.

The President of the United States had

forbidden any of its citizens to help the insurgents, but his orders were not obeyed, for there were always plenty of idle men in the larger towns glad of an excuse for a plundering excursion into Canada. Four hundred of them were met on the ice of the Detroit River by a smaller band of British regulars and driven back to their own shore. There was another fight in the same district the next year, when four hundred and fifty rebels and their friends crossed from Detroit to Windsor, and did a lot of damage on their march towards the village of Sandwich. There Colonel Prince met them with half the number of militia, and succeeded in beating them so badly that they made no more raids.

1838. The most heroic stand of the rebellion was made at Prescott in November of that year, under a brave and skilful soldier from Poland, Colonel Van Schultz. Of the six hundred men who joined him at Ogdensburg, partly "patriots" and partly American seekers of land, only one hundred and seventy reached the Canadian shore. There they were caught in a trap, for the American authorities seized their boats and they could not get back again, nor could the rest of the six hundred come to help them. Being hotly attacked, the invaders took refuge in a big stone windmill near Prescott, and held out there for three days, till regulars came from Kingston with cannon strong enough to batter down the walls. Then they gave up, and Van Shultz with eleven others was brought to trial and hanged.

1837. In Lower Canada, the rebellion took more the form of a war of races. The French Canadians, who numbered three times more than the British, thought it was not fair they should have no voice in the governing Council. Their leader was Louis J. Papineau, Speaker of the House of Assembly, who well knew how to stir up the excitable minds of his countrymen against the powers that be. He was better as a talker than a fighter, and when the "Sons of Liberty" were called to arms, it was Dr. Wolfred Nelson who commanded them. He lived at St. Denis on the Richelieu River, and before there had been any fighting in Upper Canada, a battle took place there which lasted from nine o'clock in the morning till four in the afternoon of November 23rd. The troops from Montreal, who were tired before it began with their twelve-hour march through the mud, could not drive the rebels out of the four-storied stone building in which they had placed themselves; but the victory did Nelson no good. He had not the means to keep up a war; and when his followers heard that another body of soldiers was coming against them they went home, and he made his way over the line into the States. So did Papineau.

There was another skirmish two days later in the neighbouring village of St. Charles, but the rebels ran away at the first cannon-shots. At St. Eustache, north of Montreal, some " Sons of Liberty " took possession of a stone church, and had to be burnt out of it. A final attempt to turn Lower Canada from her allegiance to Great Britain was made by a brother of Dr. Nelson in the autumn of 1838. After a fight with the Caughnawaga Indians, in which the rebels were beaten, the latter marched on to Odelltown, where it was the militia who gained the church and the insurgents were not able to put them out. As in Upper Canada, citizens came from the United States to help the " patriots," and stayed only long enough to help themselves. Priests and seigneurs stood firm for British connection, and when the leaders of the revolt had all sought safety in the States, the people soon came back to their senses.

There was no fighting in Nova Scotia nor in New Brunswick, simply because the leaders of the reform party had better judgment than to seek to gain their ends in that way. Joseph Howe, editor of the *Nova Scotian*, and a statesman who served his country honourably to the day of his death, was a very different man from William Lyon Mackenzie, of Toronto. Howe hated the rule of the few over the many just as heartily, and he too, as a member of Assembly, lifted up his voice against the oppression of his own province; but he had a cooler head than Papineau, and a keen sense of humour that helped to keep him sane. Lemuel Allan Wilmot was the leader in New Brunswick and a good speaker too, though not so witty as Howe. The plan of both men was to keep on appealing to the lawgivers at Downing Street, without breaking the laws, on the principle that constant dropping wears out a stone. The stone did wear out in the end, but its yielding was delayed by the rebellion, for of course so much talk about annexation sent all the moderate Reformers over to the Tory side.

BRITISH COLUMBIA

CHAPTER XVII

THE NEW DOMINION

1838. At length there was sent to Canada a governor-general who was clever and strong-minded enough to think for himself, and not to be ruled by Council or Family Compact. Lord Durham was only six months in the country, from May till October, but in that time he took pains to get at the root of the trouble, and he fully succeeded. Nor was he afraid, as the governors before him had been, to tell unpleasant truths to Downing Street, about how much cause Canadians had had to revolt. Great Britain had learned something by the loss of her other colonies in America and was more than willing to act upon Lord Durham's report.

In course of time each province gained her heart's desire, Responsible Government.

1840. Lord Durham's advice was also carried out in the union of Upper and Lower Canada, with Kingston for a capital. The French Canadians did not like that arrangement very well, looking upon it as a scheme for doing away with their language, laws, and religion. The English minority in Lower Canada would be turned into a majority, and have things all their own way in the Assembly, when joined by the English of Upper Canada. Before very long the Upper Canadians wanted to send more members to Parliament because they had more people than Lower Canada; but the latter would not let them. So the two provinces jogged along in an uncomfortable harness, pulling together about as well as an ox and a mule might do.

1842. French and English colonists had fought about the boundary line of Acadia; the quarrel was now between lumbermen of New Brunswick and the United States. They had come to blows in 1839, and their two Governments saw that the time had arrived when the matter must be settled. England was far away and did not care very much about it, so by the Ashburton Treaty, a handsome slice of New Brunswick was given to Maine. The

Americans were sharp enough to keep out of sight a correct map they had of the boundaries agreed upon at the Treaty of Versailles.

1849. The Canadian Parliament voted money to pay damages to those who had had property destroyed in the late rebellion; but Upper Canada objected to any of this fund going to Lower Canada, where, it was said, all the people had been rebels at heart. Montreal was having its turn of being capital, and when the governor, Lord Elgin, signed the Rebellion Losses Bill, he was mobbed in the streets. The rioters then went to the House of Parliament, turned out the members, and burned the building to the ground.

1858. That settled Montreal's fate as the capital of Canada; and Queen Victoria was asked to choose a new site, where good buildings would be erected for Parliament to meet in every year, instead of being changed from place to place as it had been. The Queen fixed upon Bytown, a small lumber village on the Ottawa River, named from Colonel By, engineer of the Rideau Canal. Neither Toronto nor Kingston, Montreal nor Quebec could be jealous of so humble a rival, and it was farther away from the frontier than any of them. The name was changed to Ottawa, which thus became the permanent capital of Canada.

The same year saw a submarine cable laid from England to Halifax, and dollars and cents used instead of pounds, shillings, and pence.

1859-1860. The next year was noted for a change in the land system of Lower Canada. The Government bought out the seigneurs and gave each habitant the chance to buy his own farm—thus doing away with the feudal system which had been in force since the settlement of the country. The lands set apart for the clergy were given up to be used for the purposes of education, and Canada has never since had an established Church. The visit of the Prince of Wales was a great event in the colony. He opened the Victoria Railway Bridge which spans the wide, swift St. Lawrence at Montreal, and is the largest tubular iron bridge in the world. His Royal Highness also laid the cornerstone of the Parliament Buildings at Ottawa.

1866. When the war between the North and South in the United States was over, a number of idle soldiers were let loose upon the country, and some of these who belonged to the Fenian Brotherhood thought that the time had come to revenge Ireland's wrongs by making a raid on Canada. The United States Government took no steps to stop them. In the month of May, one Colonel

O'Neil, with nine hundred Fenians, crossed from Buffalo in scows and made for the Welland Canal, to destroy it; but before they got there they were met at the village of Ridgeway by five or six hundred militia from Toronto and Hamilton — shopmen, clerks, and mechanics, who had never smelt powder. The 16th Regiment of British regulars was approaching from another direction, but the volunteers were in too great a hurry to wait for it. Seeing some horses' heads on the horizon, the colonel, an auctioneer from Hamilton, shouted the command, "Form square to receive cavalry!" No cavalry came of course, but those youths whose faces had been turned homewards by the stupid order, charged in that direction, and their comrades quickly did the same when fired upon by the Fenians. The invaders ran away too when they heard that the regulars were coming, and so the canal was saved.

During the next three or four years the Fenians made several trips over the Canadian border at different points from Quebec to Manitoba, but at length the officer in command of the American fort nearest to Winnipeg, on the Red River, arrested Colonel O'Neil, and his followers soon scattered.

It was in the autumn of 1864 that the first

steps were taken towards a union or confederation of all the British colonies in North America. The Maritime Provinces—Nova Scotia, New Brunswick, and Prince Edward Island—had sent delegates to meet at Charlottetown, the capital of Prince Edward Island, for the purpose of talking about a union among themselves. To this meeting came a strong deputation from the Canadas, Upper and Lower, proposing the larger scheme of uniting all the provinces, and this was further discussed at a conference held in Quebec a month later. Thirty-three delegates met there for eighteen days, and seventy-two resolutions were adopted which met with approval in Great Britain, but were not at once agreed to by the different provinces. Upper and Lower Canada were the strongest in favour of confederation, and so soon as it was settled they changed their names and became the provinces of Ontario and Quebec.

Nova Scotia was displeased because her Government agreed to confederate without taking a second vote from the people about it, and stirred up by the eloquence of Joseph Howe, still her most famous statesman, she went so far as to try to get out of the union a year after it was made. Her wounded feelings were soothed in time,

P

chiefly by the generous help given by her sister provinces at the time when a large portion of her population was brought to the point of starvation by a bad season in the fisheries. New Brunswick was not very enthusiastic, until the unfriendliness of the United States made her long for the support of the other provinces. The New Dominion of Canada, which was born on the 1st of July, 1867, is worthy of having its birthday ever remembered with pride and joy by future generations of Canadians.

From the American war the provinces learned one lesson of importance, and that was how to confederate. The trouble in the United States had arisen through the central government at Washington having too little power and each individual state too much. The thirteen English colonies had sprung up with different laws and with different kinds of colonists. Though they agreed to unite in throwing off the yoke of the mother country, they were still jealous of one another and afraid that state rights would be taken away by the central government, so they yielded no more of them than they could possibly help. Hence it came to pass that the Southern States thought they could go out of the union, whenever its plans did not please them, and for this right they fought and were defeated.

Canada, on the contrary, gave all power to the central government at Ottawa, and it decided what each province should do for itself. The building of schools, for example, and public works of all sorts; the granting of licences and the payment of taxes; the punishment of crime and the arrangement of any affairs which the various towns cannot settle for themselves—these are some of the duties of the provincial government which is stationed in the capital of each province, and has its House of Parliament on the same plan as the one at Ottawa.

The Dominion Government has control of the banks, the Post Office, the Indians and their lands, the trade between provinces and that with foreign nations, the defence of the country by land and sea, the fisheries, and any other matters that concern the Dominion as a whole. England reserves to herself the right to interfere if the Parliament at Ottawa makes laws that clash with those that the Parliament in London has made in respect to the dealings of the British Empire with other nations; but if one of those other nations should dream of conquering Canada, it would find itself face to face with the army and navy of Great Britain.

The governor-general of Canada is appointed by the Queen, for five years, and his power, like hers, is moral and social, rather than political, for he can do nothing without the consent of his Council, or cabinet of thirteen members, responsible to the people. The governor and his cabinet appoint the lieutenant-governor for each province, and also the senators, who hold office for life and correspond to the Lords of England. The judges too are appointed for life, instead of being elected, as in the United States; and it has been found that justice is more apt to be done by a man who has nothing but the right and wrong of a case to think of, than by one who is likely to be tempted to consider how his judgment will please the voters who have made him a judge and can unmake him at the next election.

Canadians proudly affirm that their government is more stable and gives more security to life and property than that of the United States. Its officials are not certain to lose their places whenever a new party comes into power, and are not therefore tempted, in the same degree, to help themselves out of the nation's pocket during the short time that they have the chance.

1873. Prince Edward Island did not come into the confederation till it had been tried for six years and proved a success. Newfoundland saw no advantage to herself in it above the Responsible Government which had been granted her, and the "Ancient Colony" prides herself in not yet being swallowed up in the Dominion. Nor is Canada overanxious for Newfoundland to join the sisterhood till she gets rid of her " French shore." Better for England to have that affair in her own hands, because it arose out of her having agreed, in the Treaty of Utrecht, to let the fishermen of France land and dry their fish, erecting stages or huts for the purpose, anywhere in the seven hundred miles between Cape St. John and Cape Ray on the west coast of Newfoundland. This agreement was made in 1713, when codfishing only was meant, but that is at an end, so far as the French shore is concerned. The industry now carried on there is lobster-catching, and permanent buildings have been put up, wherein the lobsters are boiled and tinned, ready for the market. Against the terms of the treaty, the Frenchmen engaged in this work stay on the island all the year round, and they will not let the English take part in the same business nor settle on the disputed shore, and in these claims they have been upheld by British ships of war.

France owns the two little islands of St. Pierre and Miquelon, close by, which are the most famous smuggling resorts in North America and a cause of great loss to the Canadian Customs; but the quarrel is chiefly between France and England. It is Great Britain who must demand of her neighbour across the Channel what right she has to keep her Newfoundland subjects shut out from a valuable part of their island; and to ask her also if she does not know the difference between a lobster and a cod.

MANITOBA

CHAPTER XVIII

THE NORTH-WEST

HE great lone land reaching from Lake Superior to the Rocky Mountains, at the beginning of the nineteenth century owned no rulers but the Hudson's Bay Company and its younger rival, the North-west Company. Neither of these wanted settlers to come in, nor did the Indians. The farmer was the foe to the fur trade, driving away the wild animals; and therefore the outside world was led to believe that the grassy prairies, now known to be one of the greatest wheat-growing and cattle-ranching regions of the world, was

naught but a dreary waste, unsuited for bearing crops of any kind.

The employés of the Hudson's Bay Company were mostly men from the Orkney Islands, but the North-west Company found itself better served by French Canadian *voyageurs* and half-breeds, a wild, rollicking lot, but obedient to their commanders and far more enterprising, as well as better liked by the Indians, than the staider Scotchmen. When the governor of the older Company was the Earl of Selkirk, the same who had taken out Highlanders to Prince Edward Island, he thought he could check the Nor'-westers by bringing out a number of his countrymen to settle upon the Red River, where the Assiniboine flows into it.

1811. He secured a large grant of land there, and his colonists sailed in July direct from Scotland to Hudson's Bay, the shortest sea route ; but as they were not landed until September, they got no further than Nelson River that first winter, and suffered severely from sickness and want of food. The next summer they reached Red River, only to be met by a band of Nor'-westers, painted and dressed like Indians, who warned them off the lands allotted to them and forced them to continue their toilsome journey on foot to the nearest Hudson's Bay post, which was at Pembina, in the territory of the United States. There they spent the winter, supporting themselves by hunting, and in the spring came down the Red River again. Lord Selkirk sent out more emigrants, but he neglected to send enough food with them, or implements to till the soil, so that for several seasons they had to go to Pembina for the winter.

The North-west Company continued to oppose the settlement. Twice they destroyed it by fire, and on one of those occasions killed its governor and twenty-one of his men. That outrage made Lord Selkirk bring out one hundred disbanded soldiers—French, German, and Swiss—with whom he attacked and took Fort William, the western headquarters of the rival Company. Then he brought more colonists, supplied them with farming tools, and induced the original settlers to come back. Not being of the kind which is easily discouraged, they built their log-houses over again and lived on fish, roots, and wild berries while they planted their fields once more. There were no trees to be cut down and the rich soil gave a ready return, but before the harvest ripened there came a plague of grasshoppers, which ate up every green thing in sight. The hope of winter provision was gone in a night, and once more the settlers had to take the weary tramp to Pembina. They spent the next winter there also, for the grasshoppers had left their families behind them to be fed before those of the colonists.

Out of the first eight winters that these emigrants had spent in America, they had so far been able to hold their own for only two at the Selkirk settlement; and when foes from without ceased to trouble them the Red River itself, through the jam of melting ice in the spring following an unusually severe winter, rose nine feet in a day, overflowed its banks and flooded the fields and houses. Losing heart through year after year of bad fortune, some of the settlers gave up trying to be farmers and became boatmen, hunters, or labourers for the Hudson's Bay Company. About fifty families made their way east to Toronto, but Lord Selkirk had seed-wheat carried all the way from the Mississippi to help the rest; and the foreign soldiers he had brought out settled down among them, thus making quite a mixture of nationalities in the camp.

The war between the Hudson's Bay and North-west Companies had been waged ever since the starting of the latter in

1783, but most of the fighting had been done between the employés of the two in the far-off wilds, where nobody heard about it. Lord Selkirk's attempt at making a colony brought the strife to a head, and it was kept up with great bitterness until his death. Soon after that the two became one under the government of the Hudson's Bay Company, which bought the Earl's settlement from his heirs and made their headquarters in it, at Fort Garry. None of the colonists were allowed to do any fur-trading on their own account, and they were supposed to get all the goods they needed from the Company, which in return bought their farm produce.

1821. The older Company gained much in enterprise by its union with the younger, and became more powerful than ever, with an immense staff, though scattered over so wide an extent of territory there would often be at a post only one or two white men, who were completely at the mercy of the surrounding savages; but their fair dealing kept them safe. Some of the strictest rules of the Company were that the Indians should be treated kindly, should not be cheated out of their furs, should be paid in advance for them when they had no food, powder, or shot, and should be given the smallest possible amount of strong liquor in return for the results of their winter hunts. The value of all other skins was reckoned by that of the beaver, used so much in Europe for the making of gentlemen's hats. A fox or a bear, a lynx, an ermine, or a sable, was said to be worth so many beaver skins.

The sixty thousand Indians—Assiniboines, Crees, Blackfeet, Peigans, Chipewyans, and the rest—became more and more dependent on the Hudson's Bay Company for their daily bread, as the buffalo grew scarce and they could not get enough of its flesh to dry and smoke for their winter supply of "pemmican." Once the herds had made the earth tremble with their tread as they careered over the plains, chased by Indians on horseback, who killed, just for sport, far more than they needed, and paid no attention to the laws the Company made for preserving the animal.

The Hudson's Bay Company gained respect both for itself and for the British flag under which it traded, and in its long term of rule there were no Indian wars such as spread terror through the western parts of the United States. It kept out lawless fur-traders from the south, who would have ruined the Indians with liquor, as well as speculators, who would have stolen their lands. Thus it saved the country for England and gave Canada a good lesson upon how to govern the vast territory when it came into her hands.

1869. That happened by purchase, the Company still keeping its posts and a small portion of land around each; but the change of rulers was badly managed, and directly after she had created the new province of Manitoba, the Dominion found herself with a rebellion on her hands. The leader of it was a half-breed called Louis Riel, a man of some little education and much influence with his countrymen, who looked upon him as an inspired prophet more worthy of their regard even than the clergy of the Roman Catholic Church. Canada would have done better to have explained her plans to her new subjects, and not have let herself be represented in the west by some surveyors and loud talkers, who had much to say about what they were going to do when the Red River settlement became Manitoba. The half-breeds feared they would lose their farms.

The lieutenant-governor sent from Ottawa to the new province by way of the United States, was met near the frontier by Louis Riel with a body of armed men, who had placed a barricade across the road and refused to let him come farther, so he went back to Pembina. The rebels then took possession of Fort Garry and set up what they called a provisional government, with Riel at its head. He arrested about fifty men who would not acknowledge his rule, and one of them, called Thomas Scott, he tried by a sham court-martial, and then had him shot in a most brutal manner just outside the gates of the fort. This murder set all the English-speaking people of the settlement against Riel, though many before had sympathised with the rebels, and it also raised a storm of wrath in Ontario, the province to which Scott belonged.

1870. Five hundred regular troops and seven hundred militia were sent west under Colonel Garnet Wolseley, who has since become commander-in-chief of the British army, and as it was unlawful for them to pass through the United States territory, the soldiers took the old canoe route of La Vérendrye, from the head of Lake Superior, by Rainy River and Lake of the Woods. After six hundred miles of most difficult travelling they reached Fort Garry, to find its gates standing open and the rebels gone. Lord Wolseley did not forget the skill shown by Canadian boatmen on that expedition, and when he headed another in Egypt (1884) he sent for about four hundred of them to help him at the cataracts of the Nile.

Settlers now began to pour into Manitoba, and among them came Icelanders and Mennonites, a German people who had been living in Russia. Winnipeg, the thriving young capital of Manitoba that had grown up round Fort Garry, became a university town in 1877. But the Dominion had not yet done with M. Riel. He had made his escape to the United States and become an American citizen, when the half-breeds of the North-west Territory begged him to come back and help them get their rights by force. Their farms stretched back from the Saskatchewan River in long strips, after the Quebec fashion, and they did not want surveyors to come in from Ontario and divide up the country into square blocks. They had begged the Ottawa rulers to give them good titles to their lands. They thought their district ought to be made into a province with self-government, like Manitoba, and they wanted schools and hospitals, seed - wheat and farming tools for themselves, as well as hunting grounds set apart for their Indian cousins, who looked to the half-breeds to plead their cause.

The Dominion Government had been slow in attending to these requests, which were not all unreasonable, but they were quick enough in sending out the militia to put a stop to the rebellion after it started. If Riel had succeeded in his plan of rousing all the Indian tribes of the North-west to go on the war-path, every lonely settlement would have been wiped out, if not Winnipeg itself. As it turned out, the most mischief was done by Big Bear, a chieftain of the Crees, whose followers massacred a number of people at Frog Lake. Poundmaker, also a Cree, declared afterwards that he would never have taken up the hatchet if his people had not been first attacked; and the rest of the tribes kept neutral.

1885. The first fight was at Duck Lake, between the north and south branches of the Saskatchewan, where two hundred rebels, under Gabriel Dumont (Riel's second in command and a good fighter), surprised and defeated a force, half the size, of volunteers from Prince Albert and North-west Mounted Police, the small, but well-trained body of men whose duty it is to keep order throughout that immense territory.

Riel had taken up his stand at Batoche, on the southern branch of the Saskatchewan, and there General Middleton marched to give him battle with the regiments from Ontario and Quebec who had come part of the way by the nearly completed Canadian Pacific Railway, but had still much hard travelling to do at the worst season of the year, when the snow is melting and the ice in the rivers breaking up. Before they reached Batoche they were fired upon by Gabriel Dumont and two hundred and eighty rebels who were hiding in the rifle-pits they had dug along the banks of Fish Creek. After five hours' hot fighting with Middleton's three hundred and fifty men, the half-breeds were driven from one ravine to another and fell back on Batoche, where Middleton thought it safer not to attack them till the rest of his troops arrived.

Fort Pitt, between Edmonton and Battleford, had meanwhile been taken by Big Bear's band, though the garrison of Northwest Mounted Police, led by Inspector Dickens, a son of the novelist, had made its escape in scows through the floating ice down the river to Battleford. There also were gathered about six hundred people from the neighbourhood, mostly women and children, in deadly fear of Poundmaker's tribe. Colonel Otter, with three hundred Canadian regulars and volunteers, as well as fifty mounted police, marched across the two hundred miles of prairie to the relief of Battleford, and when it was safe he marched out again to chastise Poundmaker. His men fell into an ambush laid by the Indians in the ravine, through which runs Cut Knife Creek, and after a six hours' fight they were obliged to retreat to Battleford.

The chief battle of the rebellion, and the one which ended it, was begun at Batoche on the 9th of May, by which time the ice in the river was loosened, and help could come up by steamboat from Lake Winnipeg. The Canadians had one Gatling gun, worked by an American officer, which was of great use in driving the rebels from their rifle-pits and trenches. The fight lasted for three days, and the half-breeds never stopped firing day nor night. They had many good sharp-shooters, and were mostly very brave, but at last they had to give way to superior numbers, and Batoche was taken by storm. Dumont made his escape, but Riel was taken prisoner, brought to trial for treason, and in spite of the plea of insanity and the race agitation started in his favour, he was hanged at Regina, the capital of the North-west Territories.

1890. The whole of these—Assiniboia, Saskatchewan, Alberta, and Athabasca—began to send members to Ottawa, and soon had Responsible Government of their own. The half-breeds gained most of the things they wanted, and the number of the North-west Mounted Police was increased to one thousand, so that these brave red-coated troopers have needed no more help in keeping the peace along "the far-flung fenceless prairie."

BRITISH COLUMBIA

CHAPTER XIX

BRITISH COLUMBIA

"ALEXANDER MACKENZIE from Canada by land, the twenty-second of July, one thousand, seven hundred and ninety-three."

That notice was painted up on a high cliff above the Pacific Ocean by an officer of the North-west Company, who was afterwards knighted. He had good reason to be proud of his exploit, for he was the first white man to follow the Peace River through the Rocky Mountains; the first to succeed in crossing them from the east; the first to make the dangerous and difficult journey through another unknown sea of mountains that extended to the coast; the first to reach the Pacific Ocean, still the goal of every expedition from the East, whether by land or sea. Mackenzie had tried it three years before, when he left Lake Athabasca by canoe and went north through the Slave River and Great Slave Lake into the mighty stream now called after him. He sailed to its entrance into the Arctic Ocean before he decided that the north-west passage was not to be found that way. In his overland journeys in search of the same, between the years 1819 and 1827, Sir John Franklin reached the Arctic Sea both by the Coppermine and the Mackenzie River; but when he went into the frozen north with his two ships in 1845 he never came out again, and looking both for him and for the north-west passage, Arctic expeditions became more the rage than ever. They did no good to Canada, for the tales of every returned traveller were full of icebergs, glaciers, dog-trains, and Eskimo; and it will still take many a barrel of Ontario apples and many an annual report of shows where fruits almost tropical have been exhibited, to make Europeans understand how great are the varieties of climate even within the limits of one province such as British Columbia.

1806, 1808, 1811. Acting upon the advice

of Sir Alexander Mackenzie, the North-west Company set up trading posts in New Caledonia, as the country to the west of the Rocky Mountains was then called, and the first of these appears to have been upon Lake Stuart. The man from whom it was named and Simon Fraser, the discoverer and explorer of the famous river called after him, extended their travels as far south as the Columbia River. There the Nor'-westers ere long came into contact with the South-west Fur Company, started by John Jacob Astor, of New York, whose trading post at the mouth of the Columbia was named Astoria.

After a couple of years of rivalry the Nor'-westers bought out the Astorians, but they did not long have the field to themselves, for the Hudson's Bay Company followed them over the mountains. The strife between the two was as keen as in the North-west Territories, but after their union in 1821 the Hudson's Bay Company set up new trading posts throughout New Caledonia and Oregon, which then included California and Washington Territory. Its governor, Sir George Simpson, travelled to Europe by way of Alaska and Siberia, and it was he who had the first forts built on Vancouver Island. The Company held both sides of the

Columbia, from the Rocky Mountains to the sea, and had it been backed up by the British Government the whole country from the Russian possessions, now called Alaska, down to Mexico, might have belonged to England.

1826. Little was known, or cared, in Great Britain about a land so far away; but the United States were not blind to their own interests, and they clamoured for a division of the territory. The boundary agreed upon between their possessions and those of the Hudson's Bay Company was the Columbia River; but the Company was allowed to hold its trading posts as far south as San Francisco, and having leased Alaska from the Russians, it kept them out of the fur trade, and extended its own to Behring Sea.

The headquarters were at Fort Vancouver, on the Columbia River, about twenty miles from its mouth, in the middle of a fine farming and grazing country, upon which the Americans soon cast longing eyes. They had had their own way with Great Britain in the settlement of boundaries in the east; they expected the same indulgence in the west. By claiming the whole region up to Russian America, latitude 54° 40', they might at least gain possession of the Columbia valley, so, according to their custom, they raised a popular cry : " Fifty-four Forty, or Fight !"

1846. Great Britain, far off and indifferent, gave way for the sake of peace, and at the Treaty of Oregon yielded the country, not so far as Russian America, it is true, but up to the forty-ninth parallel of latitude ; and thus was lost to Canada a large tract of country which should now be hers. There was still further difficulty about the ownership of the island of San Juan, to the south of Vancouver Island ; but the Americans got it at last.

Before the boundary disputes were settled the Hudson's Bay Company thought it safer to move its headquarters to the southern end of Vancouver Island, and there, in 1843, was built its strongest fort. It had a cedar fence twenty feet high about the buildings, and a dozen cannon mounted at the corners. That was the core around which grew Victoria, the capital of British Columbia. It sprang from a trading post into a city at one bound when gold was found in large quantities on the Fraser River and its tributary, the Thompson, named from the North-west Company surveyor who had discovered it half a century before.

1858. Twenty or thirty thousand miners trooped in among the lonely mountains of the mainland, chiefly from the California diggings, where they had known no law but the revolver. They were hard to control, but Governor James Douglas, also a chief factor of the Hudson's Bay Company, proved equal to the task, and for his strong hand in keeping order and his energy in having good roads built to open up the country for settlement he is often called "the Father of British Columbia."

1866. Vancouver Island and the mainland were under separate governments for eight years, and during that time New Westminster, on the Fraser, was the capital of the latter, but the full dignity was returned to Victoria at the union of the two, which was the first step towards the entrance of British Columbia into the Canadian Confederation. The Pacific province was not very anxious to go in. Her colonists had come direct from England, round Cape Horn or northwards from the United States; what interest had they in furthering Canada's ambition to spread herself from ocean to ocean?

Settlers from Ontario, trailing their families and effects in huge covered waggons over the plains, did well when they got as far as the prairie province, Manitoba. To the westward was a vast plain over which the Indian still roved in savage freedom, and then came the Rocky Mountains, a high wall, hard to climb, guarding the approaches to British Columbia. But the makers of the Dominion saw that unless the provinces united and presented a solid front to the encroachments of the United States, the latter would soon own all the country west of the Rocky Mountains, up to the Arctic Ocean, for they had now bought Alaska from Russia.

1867. If the British Columbians did not care particularly for Canada they cared still less about annexation. Though there was much coming and going with California by sea, the idea of taking second place to San Francisco for good did not please Victoria. The English colonists spoke out strongly in opposition to those from the United States, and determined to keep up the British connection. They would join the Canadian Confederation if Canada made it worth their while. In the first place, she must shoulder their debt of $1,500,000, which the ten thousand settlers in the province were finding a heavy burden; secondly, and most important, she must build a railway across the continent, connecting British Columbia with the Canadian railways in the east.

1871-1886. Canada accepted the terms, and accordingly began the Canadian Pacific Railway within two years from the time that the new province came into the union ; but in agreeing to finish it within ten she had promised more than she could perform. To survey miles and miles of unknown and mostly mountainous country in search of the best route ; to bridge deep canons through which gigantic rivers roar in torrents ; to tunnel through the shoulders of mountains and make safe roads along the sides of dizzy precipices ; to avoid the probable track of avalanches, and when all was done to build snow-sheds to shelter the road where the drifts were found to be deepest was a labour in which many an older and wealthier nation would have spent twenty years. Canada is proud that she completed it in fifteen. The Dominion Government undertook the task, but it was afterwards turned over to the Canadian Pacific Railway Company, which sent a through train from Montreal to Vancouver just five years after the time first appointed.

The resources of British Columbia are still so slightly developed that they seem boundless. The Fraser River has treasures other than gold with which to enrich the industrious. Countless salmon, some of them seventy pounds in weight, run up into its waters in the summer, and often there will be as many as two thousand fishing-boats about its mouth at one time, which will each take two or three hundred fish into the nets in a single night. These are for the two score of canneries on the banks of the Fraser, and there are half as many more on the smaller rivers and inlets of the coast. A tin of British Columbia salmon has become a well-known article of food in the east, but it represents only a part of her wealth in fish—she has many other varieties.

Although it is not for farming lands that the Pacific, like the prairie province, is specially noted, she has five hundred thousand acres, chiefly in the Fraser valley and on Vancouver Island, that are suitable for the purpose, and much that is now used only for grazing will in course of time be sown with grain. It was not farmers, but miners and speculators who took up the land, and the trees are so large and the undergrowth so thick it is not easily cleared. The giant Douglas fir, which along the coast lifts its head three hundred feet in the air, clear of branches till half-way up, and measures five or six feet through, is king of the

British Columbia timber, which ranks only second to her mines.

It was in the year 1851 that some Indians, watching a blacksmith at work, told him they knew where he could get more of the black stone he was using on his fire, and that remark led to the discovery of the coal mines at Nanaimo, which have been worked ever since. It looked like a special provision for the steamships which began to run to Japan in 1887, that coal should be plentiful in Vancouver Island, just as the amount of the same in Nova Scotia seems to have been stored there on purpose to supply the fast Atlantic liners.

By the building of the Canadian Pacific Railway, not only has the wilderness of the North-west been made to blossom like the rose into farms and villages, but the long-sought-for short cut to the East has been discovered. There is no stronger evidence of that fact than the number of Chinamen seen in British Columbia. Her climate, damp on the coast, dry among the mountains, will attract many more desirable colonists as the years go on, for the warm winds and currents of the Pacific Ocean make her winters milder and her summers cooler than those of any other province of the Dominion. Tourists, too, need no longer go abroad for change of air, nor for glaciers, snow-capped peaks, and other magnificent scenery. Switzerland is but a commonplace penny pamphlet compared with that new and wildly romantic three-volume novel, British Columbia.

PRINCE EDWARD ISLAND

CHAPTER XX

"DAUGHTER AM I IN MY MOTHER'S HOUSE,
BUT MISTRESS IN MY OWN"

1888. GREAT BRITAIN is beginning to realise that Canada is grown up. The day is far past when her concerns were settled by English statesmen without consulting her own. No longer can the United States get for the asking as much of her territory and as many of her fishery rights as they want. The Americans do not relish the change, and they rejected the last Washington Treaty in which Nova Scotian fishery claims might have been settled, because at length something like justice was proposed to Canadian interests.

Still less did the United States commissioners relish the decision in the

Behring Sea dispute, which was settled by arbitration in Paris (1893), for they were told that they could not claim the ocean as well as the earth, and that Canadians had a perfect right to hunt for seals in Behring Sea. Both nations bound themselves not to take the animals in the early summer, nor to use firearms in their pursuit.

While under the rule of France, the sort of man sent out by the king as governor had much to do with Canada's peace and prosperity; but after Britain gained the colony, the people came more and more to the front and the governor went more and more into the background. Since confederation it has mattered but little to Canadians, except those living in Ottawa who come in contact with him personally, what the governor-general is like, though an exceedingly clever statesman, such as Lord Dufferin, will leave his mark wherever he goes. The improvements he carried out, or suggested, while in office (1872-1878), as well as the able manner in which he spoke about Canada's needs and her future after he went home, has given him a high place in her regard. By the trip which he and Lady Dufferin took to the Pacific Coast in 1876, Manitoba was made to feel herself an important part of the Dominion and to realise what great things were expected of her; while British Columbia was charmed out of her irritation at the delay of work upon the Canadian Pacific Railway, on which all her hopes were built.

The Marquis of Lorne and the Princess Louise who succeeded (1878-1883) were acceptable rulers in a social sense, but the real power of the country rests with the prime minister at Ottawa. The man in whom the people have shown most confidence by keeping him longest in that office was Sir John A. Macdonald, a leading spirit in forming the confederation and the first premier of the New Dominion. Some acts of his Tory government in connection with the building of the Canadian Pacific Railway were not approved of, and for five years he was out of power, when Alexander Mackenzie, head of the Liberal party, took the helm; but Sir John came back, saw the great railway completed, and was premier until his death. Whatever may be said of his use or abuse of power, he did not employ it to enrich himself, for he died a poor man (1891).

By putting a high duty upon American goods, he had encouraged Canadian manufactures, and though this "National Policy" is contrary to British ideas about free trade, so long as the United States keeps up a high

R

tariff wall Canada must do the same in self-defence. But not by laws alone does she protect her borders. After confederation all the British troops were withdrawn from Canada, excepting a few at Halifax, the well-fortified city which has a cable laid to Bermuda and is the headquarters for the British navy in the North Atlantic. The same position in the North Pacific is held by Esquimault, a strongly defended harbour in British Columbia. There are a few Canadian regular soldiers at Fredericton, Quebec, Kingston, Toronto, London, and Winnipeg; but the militia is the chief defence, and the number of men between eighteen and sixty in a population bordering on five millions is not to be scorned.

1893. Those who stood on the dock at Victoria and watched the first steamship sail in from Sydney must have felt a thrill of brotherly friendship go out towards the far-off Queen of the South. The feeling will grow stronger yet when the submarine cable connects Canada and Australia, helping Greater Britain to laugh at dividing distances and to look forward with confident hope to the day when it will come into a yet closer union with Lesser Britain.

Sir John Macdonald was the first of her statesmen to make Canada feel herself no longer a colony but a nation, able not only to manage her own household but to take a hand in the management of her mother's. He was made a member of the Queen's Privy Council in 1879. Sir John Thompson, a later premier of Canada, had just received the same honour when he died, suddenly, at Windsor Castle, and his body was brought home on a warship (1894).

By the time Imperial Federation is a fact, not a sentiment, Canada will be not the least important factor in the sum. If size be taken into account, she has that; if natural products, she will then be the greatest wheat-grower among nations; nowhere else on the globe is there so much coal and timber, such valuable fisheries. Already she ranks as the fourth ship-owning country of the world, and the fresh-water highway into her very heart is not equalled anywhere. In 1895 the crown was placed upon her canal system by the opening of the one at Sault Ste. Marie, between Lakes Huron and Superior, and by the time the St. Lawrence canals are made the same depth—twenty feet—ships can sail from the ocean to the head of Lake Superior and be in Canada all the way.

1896. The year after the waste lands in the northern part of the Dominion were divided into the districts, Ungava, Franklin,

Mackenzie, and Yukon, the last-named sprang into worldwide fame by the discovery of gold on the Klondyke, a Canadian branch of the Yukon River. As usual on such occasions, there has been a frantic rush of gold-seekers, and more than the usual number of lives lost by the upsetting of boats in rivers dangerous with rapids or drifting ice ; or by cold and starvation in toiling through the snow-choked mountain passes of the sub-arctics. There is said to be more gold there than anywhere else in the world, but it is harder to get at than elsewhere, because the ground is frozen hard all the year round and has to be thawed out—no easy matter where wood and coal are so scarce. Dawson City, from which the adventurers start for the Klondyke, is called the greatest mining camp the world ever saw, but, unlike an American mining centre, it is well governed. Law and order have never lost their hold, though the district is shut out from the rest of the world for eight months in every year.

1897. French Canadians have always taken a foremost part in Dominion politics, but Sir Wilfrid Laurier is the first French Canadian prime minister. Like most of his co-patriots in public life, he is a good speaker and he was a credit to his country at the Victorian Diamond Jubilee in London. That event was celebrated by an outburst of loyalty that took the form of a public holiday with processions and speeches in every town and village of Canada.

Laurier's government marks the return to power of the Liberal party for only the second time since confederation. Its first attention was turned to the settlement of the Manitoba school question that had been gathering trouble about itself ever since the Separate Schools for Roman Catholic children were voted down by a Protestant majority in 1890. To please both parties, it has been arranged that priests and ministers alike shall be allowed to give religious instruction to the lambs of their flocks for half an hour every day in the ordinary schools, if enough of the parents desire it to make the clergymen think it worth while.

The governor-general, Lord Aberdeen, took much interest in the matter, but indeed there was nothing that concerned the Dominion in which he and the Countess were not actively interested. Lady Aberdeen will always be gratefully remembered as the founder of the Canadian branch of the National Council of Women, and for her many and varied schemes for the good of the country. The Earl of Minto, the present governor, is not a stranger to Canada. When he was Lord Melgund he served on General Middleton's staff in the second North-west Rebellion.

That Canada is beginning to have a say in her mother's house, was seen when Great Britain altered her trade treaties with Germany and Belgium at her request and for her benefit; while the Dominion in return agreed to favour the entrance into her markets of British goods above those of any other nation. Another sign of the times was the introduction of the Imperial Penny Postage Stamp, on Christmas Day, 1898, making it cost no more to send a letter from Canada to London, England, than to London, Ontario.

1899. It was in 1897 that the British Association for the Advancement of Science met in Canada for the second time. One of the gentlemen there present, Prince Koropotkin, visited the North-west and was much impressed with Mennonite settlement there. He wrote an account of his trip in an English magazine when he went home, and was asked shortly afterwards if Manitoba would not make a suitable home for the Doukhobors of Southern Russia, who were being fiercely persecuted for their religion. The result has been the arrival in Canada of seventy-five hundred of these peculiar people, who are like the Quakers in believing it wrong to take up arms against a fellow-man. They are hardy, honest peasants, well worthy of the help the Dominion Government is giving them, and they will do more for the future of Manitoba than any number of gold-seekers.

The strongest nations have been built up with a mixture of races, and the time is at hand when French and English will remember only that they are Canadians, will glory alike in the deeds that the ancestors of either tongue have done upon this continent, and, resolving not to be unworthy of the noble heritage left them, will look hopefully into the future, will

" Greet the unseen with a cheer."

INDEX

ABENAKIS, Indians, 5, 117, 118
Abercrombie, General, 137, 138, 140, 145
Aberdeen, Lord and Lady, 245
Acadians, 113, 116, 120, 121, 122, 125, 126
Aix-la-Chapelle, Treaty of, 125
Albanel, Father, 86
Alberta, Territory of, 226
Alexander, Sir William, 44, 47
Algonquin, Indians, 5, 6, 7, 51, 52, 53, 69, 70, 71, 73, 93, 94
Allouez, Father, 87
Americus Vespucius, 23
Amherst, General, 141, 149, 160, 163
Argall, Samuel, Captain, 43, 44, 63
Argenson, Vicomte d', 75, 78
Arnold, Benedict, Colonel, 169, 170, 171, 172, 173
Ashburton Treaty, 205
Assiniboia, Territory of, 226
Assiniboine Indians, 220
Athabasca, Territory of, 226
Avaugour, Baron d', 78

BARCLAY, Captain, 188
Batoche, Battle of, 226
Béarn, Regiment of, 138
Beauharnois, Marquis de, 110
Berry, Regiment of, 138
Biencourt, 43, 44, 57, 63
Bienville, Le Moyne de, 108, 109
Bigot, Intendant, 113, 141, 147, 148, 161, 195
Big Bear, Cree Chief, 224

Biloxi, 108
Blackfeet, Indians, 5, 220
Black Watch, Regiment, 137, 138, 163
Boscawen, Admiral, 141, 144
Bougainville, 150, 152, 155, 160
Bouquet, Henry, Colonel, 163, 164
Braddock, General, 130, 131, 146
Bradstreet, Colonel, 145, 163
Brébeuf, Father, 65, 71
Breda, Treaty of, 48, 116
British Columbia, 11, 174, 175, 193, 229, 233-238, 241
Brock, Sir Isaac, 181, 183, 184

CABOT, John, 20, 21, 22, 43
Cabot, Sebastian, 20, 21, 22
Callières, Governor, 105, 106
Canadian Pacific Railway, 225, 235, 237, 241
Cape Breton, 16, 20, 22, 110, 121, 122, 124, 144, 176, 194
Carillon. *See* Ticonderoga
Carleton, Sir Guy, 166, 169, 170, 171, 173, 177
Carignan-Salières, Regiment of, 79
Caughnawaga Indians, 106, 187, 202
Cartier, Jacques, 24-33, 38, 193
Cayugas, Indians, 6
Céloron de Bienville, 128
Champlain, Samuel de, 37-41, 49-61, 63, 64, 66, 71, 79, 80
Charnisy, d'Aulnay, 45, 46, 47
Chateauguay, Battle of, 189

249 S

INDEX

Chipewyans, Indians, 220
Chrystler's Farm, 189
Church, Benjamin, Colonel, 120
Columbus, Christopher, 14, 19, 20, 23
Cook, Captain, 174
Cortereal, Gaspar, 21, 22
Courcelle, Governor, 81, 86, 89
Coureurs de bois, 76, 86, 97, 103, 109, 111
Craig, Sir James, 180, 181
Crees, Indians, 5, 220, 224
Cut Knife Creek, Battle of, 226

DANIEL, Father, 71
Daulac, Adam, 73
Davis, John, 33
De Monts, 38, 40, 41, 49, 53, 62
Denonville, Governor, 94, 95
Detroit, 103, 104, 162-164, 182, 183, 185, 188, 200
Dickens, Inspector, N. W. M. P., 225
Dieskau, Baron, 132
Dollard. *See* Daulac
Dollier de Casson, Father, 83, 84
Donnacona, 27, 28, 30, 31
Dorchester, Lord, 178. *See* Sir Guy Carleton.
Douglas, James, 233
Doukhobors, 246
Drake, Sir Francis, 33
Drucour, Chevalier de, 144, 147
Duchesneau, Intendant, 90
Dufferin, Lord, 240
Du Lhut, 92, 103
Dumont, Gabriel, 224, 225, 226
Durham, Lord, 204, 205
Duquesne, Fort, 130, 131, 145, 146
Duquesne, Marquis, 129

ELGIN, Lord, 206
Ericson, Leif, 15, 16
Eric the Red, 14, 15
Eskimos, 2, 3, 17, 229

FAMILY Compact, The, 195, 197, 204
Fenians, 207, 208
Fish Creek, Battle of, 225
Fitzgibbon, Colonel, 187, 188, 198
Five Nations, or Six Nations, Indians. *See* Iroquois.
Forbes, Brigadier, 146, 163
Fox, Indians, 104, 134
Francis the First, 22, 25, 32

Franciscans. *See* Récollets
Franklin, Sir John, 229
Fraser, Simon, 230
Frobisher, Martin, 33
Frontenac, Governor, 89, 90, 92-95, 97-100, 105, 106
Fuca, Juan de, 34

GALINÉE, Father, 84, 85
Ghent, Treaty of, 191
Giffard, 77
Gilbert, Sir Humphrey, 34
Greenland, 2, 14, 18
Guienne, Regiment of, 138

HABITATION DE QUEBEC, 50, 51, 58
Haldimand, General, 160, 173
Half-breeds, 221, 223, 225, 226, 227
Harvey, Colonel, 187
Head, Sir Francis Bond, 198
Hearne, Samuel, 165
Hébert, 57
Hennepin, Father, 90, 92
Henry the Fourth of France, 36, 43
Hochelaga, 28, 29, 31
Howe, Hon. Joseph, 203, 209
Howe, Lord, 137
Hudson's Bay Company, 86, 100, 112, 113, 165, 174, 215, 216, 218, 219, 220, 221, 230, 231, 233
Hudson, Henry, 42
Huguenots, 38, 41, 45, 58, 62, 109
Hull, General, 182
Huron Indians, 6, 7, 28, 52, 53, 55, 56, 58, 64, 65, 66, 68, 71, 72, 73, 86, 87, 103

IBERVILLE, Pierre le Moyne d', 99, 100, 107, 108
Icelanders, 223
Indians, 1-12, 19, 67, 215, 237
Iroquois, Indians, 5, 6, 7, 29, 52, 53, 56, 69-74, 80, 83, 86, 89, 90, 93, 94, 95, 98, 99, 101, 103, 104, 106, 107, 133, 164

JESUITS, 43, 63, 64, 66, 67, 68, 71-75, 78, 84-86, 90, 93, 94, 111, 117, 168
Jogues, Father, 72
Johnson, Sir William, 132, 133, 161, 164
Joliet, Louis, 84, 87
Joncaire, 107

INDEX

KIRKE, Admiral, 59, 60
Klondyke, 244

LA BARRE, Governor de, 93, 94
Labrador, 2, 16, 25
Lachine, Massacre of, 95
La Galissonière, Comte de, 127
La Jonquière, Marquis de, 113, 127, 129
Lalemant, Father, 65, 71
La Mothe-Cadillac, 103, 109
Languedoc, Regiment, 138
La Peltrie, Madame de, 68, 69
La Reine, Regiment, 138
La Roche Dallion, 65
La Roche, Marquis de, 35, 37
La Salle, Robert Cavalier de, 83-85, 87-96, 104, 107, 108, 112, 113
La Sarre, Regiment, 138
La Tour, Charles de, 43-47
La Tour, Claude de, 44, 45
Laurier, Sir Wilfrid, 244, 245
Laval, Bishop, 74-79, 90, 93, 100
La Vérendrye, Pierre Gaultier de, 111, 112, 113, 222
Le Caron, Father, 64, 65
Le Jeune, Father, 68
Le Loutre, Abbé, 125
Le Moyne, Charles, 99, 107
Léry, Baron de, 22, 36
Lévis, Chevalier de, 136, 147, 148, 150, 154, 155, 157-160
Lorne, Marquis of, 241
Loudoun, Lord, 134
Longueuil, 107
Louis XIV., 79, 94, 108, 109, 118
Louis XV., 140
Louisbourg, 122-125, 141-145, 147
Louisiana, 93, 104, 109, 147, 161, 164
Lundy's Lane, Battle of, 190

MACDONALD, Sir John A., 241, 242
Macdonell, Major, 186
Mackenzie, Alexander, 241
Mackenzie, Sir Alexander, 228, 230
Mackenzie, William Lyon, 196-199, 203
Macnab, Sir Allan, 199
Maisonneuve, 69, 70
Mance, Mlle., 70
Manitoba, 208, 221, 223, 234, 240, 245, 246, 247
Markland, 16
Maricourt, 107
Marie de l'Incarnation, 69
Marquette, Father, 87

Masse, Father, 65
Meares, Captain, 175
Medicine Men, 67
Membertou, 40, 42, 63
Mennonites, 223, 246
Mézy, Governor, 78
Michilimackinac, 87, 103, 162, 182
Micmac, Indians, 5, 40, 63, 117, 125
Middleton, General, 224, 225, 246
Minto, Earl of, 245
Mohawk, Indians, 6, 56, 72, 80, 81, 133, 174, 180, 187
Molson, John, 192
Montcalm, Marquis de, 132-138, 147, 148, 150-154
Montgomery, General, 168-171
Montmagny, Governor, 66, 69, 75
Montagnais, Indians, 5, 51, 52, 65, 68
Moravian Town, Battle of, 189
Mound-builders, 4
Murray, General, 155-158, 160, 166

NATIONAL Policy, 241
Nelson, Doctor Wolfred, 201, 202
New Brunswick, 5, 116, 176, 183, 193, 194, 202, 203, 205, 209, 210
Newfoundland, 16, 22, 25, 26, 34, 40, 48, 100, 121, 122, 193, 213, 214
Neutral Indians, 6, 65, 84
Nicolet, Jean, 65
Northmen, or Norsemen, 14-19
North-West Company, 174, 215-218, 228, 230, 232
North-West Mounted Police, 224, 225, 227
Nova Scotia, 5, 16, 22, 115, 116, 122, 125, 176, 183, 194, 202, 209, 237, 239

OJIBWA, Indians, 5, 162
Oneida, Indians, 6
Onondaga, Indians, 6, 72, 107
Ontario, Province of, 5, 209, 223, 233
Oregon, Treaty of, 232
Ottawa, Indians, 5, 103, 161, 162
Otter, Colonel, 225
Outagamies. *See* Fox Indians.

PAPINEAU, Louis J., 201-203
Peigan, Indians, 220
Perrot, Nicholas, 87
Pepperrell, William, 123
Perry, Commodore, 188
Phips, Sir William, 98, 100, 116
Picquet, Abbé, 128
Pitt, William, 140, 141

Plains of Abraham, Battle of the, 151, 152, 153
Pontgravé, 37-40, 49
Pontiac, 161, 163
Portuguese, 19
Poundmaker, 224, 226
Poutrincourt, Baron de, 38-44, 63
Prevost, Sir George, 181, 186, 191
Prince of Wales in Canada, 207
Prince, Colonel, 200
Prince Edward Island, 26, 110, 121, 125, 176, 209, 213, 216
Proctor, General, 188

QUEBEC ACT, 166, 167, 169, 177
Quebec, Province of, 5, 208, 209, 223
Queenston Heights, Battle of, 183, 184

RAMESAY, 155
Rebellion Losses Bill, 206
Récollets, 64, 65, 85, 90
Relations, Jesuit, 68, 83
Revolution, French, 141, 177
Richmond, Duke of, 195
Ridgeway, Battle of, 208
Riel, Louis, 221-224, 226
Roberval, 32, 33
Rogers, Robert, Captain, 133, 137
Royal Roussillon, Regiment, 138
Ryswick, Treaty of, 100

SACS, Indians, 105, 134, 162
Saskatchewan, Territory of, 226
Scott, Thomas, 222
Secord, Laura, 187
Selkirk, Earl of, 216-219
Seneca, Indians, 6, 71, 83, 107, 164
Shawnese Indians, 180
Sheaffe, General, 184
Simcoe, Colonel, 177, 178
Simpson, Sir George, 230
Sioux, Indians, 111
Spaniards, 4, 21, 51, 88, 175
Stadacona, 27, 28, 29, 31
St. Castin, Baron de, 118
Ste. Foye, Battle of, 158, 159

St. Germain-en-Laye, Treaty of, 45
Stoney Creek, Battle of, 187
St. Vallier, Bishop, 101
Sulpician, Order of Priests, 77, 84, 85

TALON, Intendant, 81, 82, 85, 86
Tecumseh, 180, 182, 189
Thompson, Sir John, 243
Ticonderoga, 137-139, 168
Tracy, Marquis de, 79, 80, 81
Tonty, Henri de, 91, 92, 93, 96, 107, 108
Tuscaroras, Indians, 107

UNITED EMPIRE LOYALISTS, 174, 175, 176, 196, 198
Ursulines, 69, 156
Utrecht, Treaty of, 102, 121, 213

VAN SCHULTZ, Colonel, 200, 201
Vancouver, George, Captain, 175
Vaudreuil, Philippe de, 105, 110, 118, 119
Vaudreuil, Pierre Francois Rigaud de, 132, 136, 148, 152, 154, 155
Verchères, Madeleine de, 99
Verrazano, 22, 25, 43
Victoria, Queen, 196, 206
Viel, Nicholas, Father, 65
Vincent, General, 186, 187
Vinland, 16, 17, 18
Voyageurs. *See Coureurs de bois*

WALKER, Admiral, 105, 106
Washington, George, 129
Washington, Treaty, 239
Welland Canal, 193, 208
William Henry, Fort, 132, 134, 135, 137
Wilmot, Lemuel Allan, 203
Wolfe, James, General, 143, 149, 150, 152, 153, 155, 156, 166
Wolseley, Lord, 222

ZENO, 18

www.ingramcontent.com/pod-product-compliance
Lightning Source LLC
Chambersburg PA
CBHW032204230426
43672CB00011B/2510